MALCOLM AND ME

How to Use the Baldrige Process to Improve Your School

RICHARD E. MAURER
SANDRA COKELEY PEDERSEN

ScarecrowEducation
Lanham, Maryland • Toronto • Oxford
2004

Published in the United States of America
by ScarecrowEducation
An imprint of The Rowman & Littlefield Publishing Group, Inc.
4501 Forbes Boulevard, Suite 200, Lanham, Maryland 20706
www.scarecroweducation.com

PO Box 317
Oxford
OX2 9RU, UK

British Library Cataloguing in Publication Information Available

Library of Congress Cataloging-in-Publication Data

Maurer, Richard E.
Malcolm and me : how to use the Baldrige process to improve your school / Richard E. Maurer, Sandra Cokeley Pedersen.
p. cm.
ISBN 1-57886-030-X (pbk. : alk. paper)
1. Total quality management in education—United States—Handbooks, manuals, etc. 2. School improvement programs—United States—Handbooks, manuals, etc. 3. Malcolm Baldrige National Quality Award. I. Cokeley Pedersen, Sandra, 1956– II. Title.
LB2806 .M372 2004
371.2—dc21

2003012597

∞™ The paper used in this publication meets the minimum requirements of American National Standard for Information Sciences—Permanence of Paper for Printed Library Materials, ANSI/NISO Z39.48-1992.
Manufactured in the United States of America.

CONTENTS

ACKNOWLEDGMENTS

The concepts presented in this story are the results of much talent and hard work among some of the best educators anywhere—the faculty, staff, and board of the Pearl River School District. Their work ethic, energy, and commitment to students are unparalleled. They truly epitomize the concept of continuous improvement. Because we did not want to overlook anyone, we chose to not mention individuals by name. Each and every one of you—masterful teacher, creative administrator, dedicated support staff, or committed board member—knows who you are. You are the reason for Pearl River's success.

We would also like to acknowledge our spouses and our children for their patience during those countless evening and weekend hours we spent at our home computers over the years—writing not only *Malcolm and Me* but the many Baldrige applications that preceded this story. Then there were the late afternoons and evenings in the office writing and rewriting sections, poring through data, and formulating countless tables, charts, and graphs. You cannot take back time. Thank you for understanding the importance of this work.

We also extend a final thanks to the staff of the Malcolm Baldrige National Quality Program. Your staunch commitment to only the highest standards drives excellence. Your professional and competent support went and continues to go a long way toward keeping us focused on our journey and our number one customers—our students!

INTRODUCTION

Malcolm and Me is for you if you have wondered if your school building or school district can ever get it right and focus on education. It is written for teachers, administrators, school staff, and board members who have had the vision that perhaps things in their job can be organized differently—with the focus on improving student achievement. Whether you are a veteran teacher, an administrator who has been disillusioned over the years, or a newly hired educator who is eager to begin your life's work, you will enjoy reading this book. Perhaps you are neither newly hired nor burned out but are reading this book to see if there are some new ideas that can make you more effective in your job. You will find in the stories in this book hundreds of enriching ideas to improve your profession, whether it be delivering instruction or managing and leading a school building or district.

Malcolm and Me employs the processes developed through the Malcolm Baldrige National Quality Award program. Specifically, it talks about the seven criteria that when implemented and integrated successfully will improve student achievement and improve overall organizational performance. These performance-excellence criteria are presented in a framework that can be applied to any school classroom, building, or district. They are not presented as how-to techniques but rather as applied real-life situations with which everyone is familiar.

The seven criteria are leadership, strategic planning, student and market focus, information and analysis, faculty and staff satisfaction, process management in the classroom and in the business office, and, of course, results. Taken together and linked in terms of focus on improving student achievement, you will see dramatic change in your job productivity.

Malcolm and Me uses a story format about the experiences of a student named Malcolm and his teacher, William. It explores how these individuals and their interrelation with others are affected by a school organization that successfully employs the seven criteria of the Malcolm Baldrige program. When you meet these individuals and understand how they connect, you will discover how the seven Baldrige criteria are brought to life in a real school setting. You will see how the school district, the school building, and the teacher adapt the criteria to meet their needs. As a result, the professionals feel better about their roles and are more effective and student achievement improves.

Each chapter presents a different Baldrige category as our characters journey through the school year. At the conclusion of each chapter, there is an essential question. Similar to curriculum designs, these questions ask the reader to move beyond the story narrative and look at the big picture. The analysis here allows the reader to reflect on what is really important in employing the specific criterion.

For those interested in learning more about the Baldrige process as a means to improve their school or to seek the national award, an appendix provides a guide for getting started. In addition, we have included a self-assessment checklist provided by Baldrige to help you measure where your classroom, building, or district is in terms of implementing the seven criteria.

So, let us begin our Baldrige journey where it should begin—with our new teacher being interviewed for a teaching position.

1

BILL'S INTERVIEW: IT'S ALL ABOUT PEOPLE

FACULTY AND STAFF FOCUS

Bill nervously sat in the outer office waiting to see the superintendent of schools. It had been a long process of interviews to reach this point. He was hoping to become one of the new middle school math teachers in the Blue Fields School District.

Twice, a committee of administrators, teachers, parents, and students had interviewed him. Students had never interviewed him before. He still was unsure whether his responses to their questions about homework had been the right ones. He wondered why students were allowed to be part of the interview process. In addition, he had to teach a math class. The principal and another math teacher from the department sat in the back. The lesson went well, he thought. What he thought mattered less, he knew, than what the principal thought. He wondered if he could have done a better job if he had had more time with the students or if he had known them. Yet, here he was now, waiting to see the superintendent, so he knew something went well.

While Bill was waiting, he saw a rather large sign on the wall stating the district mission: "Every Child Can and Will Learn." That was nice, he thought. His school had a similar statement but he could not recall it exactly. Under the mission statement were the district goals. There were three.

- Improve academic performance
- Improve how the district is perceived by incorporating quality principles and values in all areas of operations
- Maintain fiscal stability and improve cost-effectiveness

Bill thought about these goals. Why three? Did his present district have goals? If they did he was not aware of them. Overall, the sign was very attractive and big. It looked nice in the lobby.

Just as he was getting more nervous and thinking, "When is this guy going to see me?" the superintendent came out and greeted him.

"Hi, William. I'm Dr. Johnston, the superintendent. Thanks for coming. Sorry to keep you waiting."

"Oh, I was just reading your material here. Thanks. Glad to meet you. Ah, oh . . ."

"Please come with me," Dr. Johnston replied.

"Sure," Bill responded and followed the superintendent into the office.

The superintendent's office was a short distance but it seemed like a walk to eternity. Bill's nervousness was raging. He thought about his answers to previous questions and was confident about them. It was those questions he was unprepared for that bothered him the most.

After they were seated, the superintendent began. "So, tell me a bit about yourself, William, and why you want a job in the Blue Fields School District."

OK, so far so good, he thought. Bill responded by giving a brief description of his teaching and training record. He was confident about this and it showed.

"William, you sound very sure of yourself as a professional teacher. I notice you have two years' experience teaching math and have done quite well. The report I heard from the high school principal stated that she was very positive about your demo lesson. You did a good job."

"Thanks, I felt it went well." Really, Bill did not want to tell him his doubts about the demo. But he was reassured that his self-confidence showed in the interview.

"William, can you tell me how you felt about the demo lesson when you were done?" Dr. Johnston asked.

OK, here it comes Bill thought. "Well, I liked the students. I wished I could have had more time with them, though."

"If you had, what would you have done differently?" Dr. Johnston leaned toward Bill.

"I'm not sure," Bill responded. "I guess I could have outlined the lesson more to meet their levels of ability. Forty minutes is not enough time."

"Sure, I know it's a contrived situation, sort of. But I like your response," Dr. Johnston replied, sitting back in his chair. Bill felt a bit more relaxed now also. Apparently his response was appropriate. The superintendent continued, "Have you ever heard of multiple intelligences, either in grad school or professional courses?"

"I have heard the term, but to be frank I'm not sure what it means. . . . Is it something to do with learning styles?"

"Yes, it is," Dr. Johnston responded. "It sounded like you practice it or try to but perhaps don't know why or precisely how. It was developed by Howard Gardner and basically states that intelligence is not one number but that there are multiple types of intelligences. People are talented and gifted in a number of different areas, not just one. Therefore, to identify and build on this variety it is important that teachers teach to the different learning styles that the students have."

"I have heard of Howard Gardner," Bill responded. Actually, he could not remember where or when but he felt it best to say something.

"Don't worry about the theory, William," Dr. Johnston said. "If you teach here we will teach you how to implement it and how we differentiate instruction for our students." Bill could not *not* worry, but Dr. Johnston seemed sincere in his statement. He was relieved, somewhat.

Dr. Johnston then handed Bill what appeared to be a bookmark. Dr. Johnston explained, "William, this is a short form of what we are all about. You can see that here we have our mission statement." Bill remembered reading this in the lobby while he was waiting. Dr. Johnston explained what it meant and how a committee of teachers, parents, students, and representatives from the community about ten years ago had formed this statement. He said it was simple in form but had a deep meaning. The district employees believe it. Bill tried to remember his district's mission statement but could not. He hoped that Dr. Johnston would not ask.

"William, do you know your district's mission statement?" Dr. Johnston asked. Uh oh, Bill had been afraid of this. "Well, I remember seeing it, but to be frank it's so long that I can't remember it all."

"I'm not surprised, William," said Dr. Johnston. "Many organizations develop these statements but that's where they end. No one knows what it is or what it stands for. Here in our district you could ask any employee what the mission is and they can tell you. It is not because we are special or that we have a fancy statement. We all know it because we review it continually. At every superintendent's conference day this mission is displayed. Our new teachers and staff are introduced to it as well."

Bill thought that at the very least the mission statement was important here in Blue Fields.

Next, Dr. Johnston said, "William, do you see the three district goals listed here under the mission statement? These are important to us as well. We don't have many goals but what we do have are important. You could stop any employee in the parking lot and ask them what the three goals are and they can tell you."

Bill reflected that he could not recall any goals that his district had. He knew there were things to do every year such as serving on beautification committees or budget awareness committees or textbook adoption committees but these did not seem as if they were the kinds of goals Dr. Johnston was talking about. Bill knew he had many projects to do each year and he knew each was as important as the other. He hoped Dr. Johnston would not ask him what his present district goals were.

"Don't worry, William, I won't ask you what your district's goals are." Bill sighed in relief. "I do want you to know that we measure each of our goals each year. We have data to back up what we did or did not do. We share this data at each superintendent's conference day and at faculty meetings and at department meetings. We share the good, the bad, and the ugly. For example, when I put the results of the recent positive gains in the fourth-grade state language-arts assessment on the screen, the teachers clapped. I then asked the kindergarten teachers to stand up. The other teachers clapped for them. It is this emphasis on line of sight that is important to us. It isn't just the fourth-grade teachers who did well but also all the staff who contributed over the years to this positive growth in student achievement. We report on the success we had attaining all three goals at each meeting. The staff knows what we have done."

Bill thought that the superintendent conference days in this district were very different from the ones he had attended. He could see that Dr. Johnston did place a lot of emphasis on data to support the goals. He could see why the goals are known in this district. Everyone seems to participate in them. Bill nodded his understanding and approval.

"William, I want you to turn the tab over. You'll find a list of eight values. These are values here at Blue Fields that we feel support our attainment of district goals."

Bill turned over the tab and started to read the values. My, he thought, there is much about this district I need to learn.

Dr. Johnston said, "William, you do not have to read them all now but if you work here you will find that these are prized. I want you to notice the first, however."

Bill read, "Our students are our customers and the product we deliver is to allow them to achieve to their highest potential."

"William, this took much discussion among the staff," Dr. Johnston said. "We had to define whom we served. Was it the taxpayers, the parents, the staff, or others? Ultimately we decided we are here because of the students. I know this statement sounds like we're running a business. In fact, we are. Everything we do is to help students learn."

Bill had never thought of students as customers but it made sense. He hoped that the district did not forget the teachers. Bill thought that if he worked here in Blue Fields for the next twenty or thirty years, he would want to be sure teachers were important. Bill asked, "What role do teachers have in these values? Where does the staff fit in?"

"I am glad you asked that, William," Dr. Johnston replied. "If you look at value six, it reads 'District employees are highly valued resources.'

"This is not just stuff on paper, William," Dr. Johnston said. "We survey our staff each year to determine the level of satisfaction. The data from this survey help us develop goals each year."

"What have you found out?" Bill asked.

"Well, that is a short question with a long answer," Dr. Johnston replied. "We disaggregate our survey data by building and among staff. For example, the secretaries at the high school have their results, the custodians have theirs, and the teachers, and so forth. The data is cut fine so we can pinpoint levels of satisfaction."

"So this is why the district can address problem areas right away," Bill said. He thought, They probably don't release the "bad" data, but he kept this thought to himself.

"Right," Dr. Johnston replied. "I present the highlighted results to the entire staff each September at the first superintendent's conference day. Of course, I can't present it all but I show the full story. Copies of the results are available in the school offices for folks to look at. And, you know, there are folks who do. We hide nothing. I believe the staff knows this and that is why we get such a high response rate for the surveys."

This is amazing, Bill thought. He could not remember if in his present district anyone in administration asked for his opinion, let alone shared it with others. This district believes in the values listed here.

"Further," Dr. Johnston said, "we devote a considerable amount of our resources to providing staff development. We will help you learn to be a better teacher than you are now. I'm not saying you're a poor teacher. You wouldn't be here if we thought that were the case. Quite the contrary, we see in you the potential to become even better. All of our new teachers are required to take five core courses. These are new-teacher orientation, using data to drive instruction, differentiated instruction, using technology as a tool in the classroom, and for teachers who have been with us for three or so years, an advanced teacher-instruction course."

"I would be interested in these courses. They would help me," replied Bill. He thought that was another example of how the district valued its teachers. Blue Fields actually puts into practice what they say they should do.

"William, if you work here you will understand that what goes on in the classroom is the single most important thing we do here. I have an important job. But it really pales in comparison with what a teacher does every day," Dr. Johnston said.

Bill thought that this was a powerful statement. He hoped it was actually true. However, it seemed that all Dr. Johnston said about mission, goals, and values was consistent with the belief that the classroom was important. He felt it took a strong leader to believe this and to make others believe it.

Dr. Johnston sensed Bill's reflection and saw him nodding approval. "William," he said, "if there were one thing I wished, one thing I could put on the outside of each school building, it would be the statement 'What we do in the classroom is the most important thing we do here in the Blue Fields School District.'"

What could Bill say? Internally, he wished he could say hooray! But Bill kept his professional composure and only nodded and smiled a lot. He wondered, if the superintendent felt this strongly about value six, how do they support the other seven values listed on the tab he was holding? Clearly, there was much to learn about this place, more than he could grasp in this interview.

Dr. Johnston looked at Bill and said, "I tell you all this, William, because if you want to work in this district you have to come to believe as passionately as all of us in our mission, goals, and values. We ask that you not just give them lip service but that over time you demonstrate to us that you believe them. If you don't think you can do this then we ask you not to consider Blue Fields as a place to work. Do you understand?"

William was sure he understood and was ready to take on the challenge. He wanted to keep his cool in the interview, so he said, "Yes, I believe I can." But he wanted to stand up and shout, "Finally, a place where what I do is considered important!"

"OK," said Dr. Johnston, "let's proceed with the rest of the interview."

Bill and Dr. Johnston then talked about Bill's qualifications, the nature of the job, the main points of the teacher contract, the benefits, and finally what salary would be offered.

Dr. Johnston was impressed with Bill and felt he was a perfect selection to teach middle school math. He said, "William, I am prepared to offer you the job. Do you want it?"

Bill enthusiastically said, "Yes," smiled, and he and Dr. Johnston shook hands.

Essential Question: Why Is the Initial Interview So Important?

Baldrige stresses the need to allow all faculty and staff to develop to their full potential within the organization. This is the essence of one of the Baldrige categories and one of the eight values Bill read on the bookmark Dr. Johnston gave him. How a school building or school district builds and maintains a work environment that allows this kind of professional growth is important. In particular, you need to look at how cooperation among employees allows innovation and initiative, how the district culture and values are communicated to staff, and how faculty and staff feedback are incorporated into the system. Faculty training and development, as well as satisfaction, are critical criteria to ensure the organization focuses on the workforce.

Research consistently demonstrates that strong schools have established trust and mutual respect between teachers and administrators. The interview sets the stage for future teacher expectations. How the administrator inquires about a teacher's view of his or her own teaching sends a strong message that teaching and learning are important in the school district. The argument can be made that a new teacher is so anxious to get a job, any job, that the emphasis the administrator places on instruction could be lost in a flurry of anxiety and the need to say the right thing. However, all candidates seeking a teaching position will walk away from an interview and reflect on what happened. After lingering doubts about what should or should not have been said, the candidate will come to an overall conclusion or feeling about an interview. What is important is that candidates feel that the administration will trust and respect them as individuals. This feeling will set the stage for the teacher's professional growth and students' achievement.

The opposite feeling can easily be set. If candidates feel that they were not listened to or that the administrator's questions were not focused on what they can do as a teacher, they may feel that they are not respected. They may feel that they are just a body to fill the classroom. The future success of these candidates is in jeopardy when this feeling of abandonment shows up in student achievement results.

Obviously, one interview does not cover all these elements nor does it transform a candidate into a good teacher. A continuous and sustained process over time will ensure that faculty and staff needs are met. It is the task of the school district to provide opportunities to teachers to become better at their craft and continue their growth. Dr. Johnston has started the process for William. Let's see in future chapters how the district meets the challenge.

2

MALCOLM'S NEW SCHOOL: START IN THE MIDDLE

STUDENT AND STAKEHOLDER SATISFACTION

Malcolm woke up anxious. He was starting in a new school today—not an easy thing for an eighth grader. His mom had moved to a new apartment in the Blue Fields School District. Blue Fields had the reputation of being the best school district in the area, and Malcolm's mom wanted him to go to a school that would help him get into a good college and get a good job.

This made Malcolm nervous. Not only did he worry about having to make new friends, he was worried about whether this new school would be too hard. Malcolm had always been an average student, getting mostly Bs and a few As. This past year, though, was more challenging for him, especially in math. He wondered if the kids at Blue Fields were smarter or if they got a lot more work.

Malcolm's mom, Jeannie, visited a lot of schools and asked a lot of questions about all of them before deciding on Blue Fields. She found out that the kids in Blue Fields had higher scores on their tests. They had fewer kids drop out of school and more of them went to college or vocational school than in the other school districts. Malcolm couldn't help but think that this was because they had more homework or longer classes or harder teachers—a troublesome thought.

After getting dressed, he met his mom in the kitchen. Jeannie was already dressed for work and was toasting a bagel for him. "So, how are you doing?" she asked Malcolm.

"Not great," he replied. "I really wish we could have just stayed where we were."

"I know you do," she said. "We've been through this before. These first couple of days will be the hardest. I know it's scary meeting new kids, but in the long run, this is so much better for you."

"I know, Mom," said Malcolm, somewhat dejectedly. "But, if this school is supposed to be so good, how much harder is the work going to be? I was keeping up fine in my old school. What if I have two or three hours of homework every night?"

This took Jeannie by surprise. They had had many talks about his schoolwork, and except for math, he never seemed particularly challenged or worried about doing well.

From her research, she knew that Blue Fields provided a highly supportive environment for all students to be successful. The school and the district had an excellent reputation, not only for their students' achievements but among the parents and community as well. She learned that they used what they called a continuous-improvement model to run their schools. Evidently, this model helped them improve their students' grades so that they could get into better colleges and vocational schools. Whenever the local newspapers published the state test scores, the Blue Fields district students always had the highest scores.

They also had lots of activities for students and were constantly trying to include kids in sports and clubs. She had talked to the PTA president and a few of the other moms, and they all said good things about the school. They liked how the teachers and administrators treated them and felt as though their concerns were heard and acted upon. Right now, though, Jeannie's concern was her son.

"Well, you know, Malcolm, I asked a lot of questions about Blue Fields when we were looking for a new school," she reminded him. "From what they told me, it seems the teachers and the other staff in the school really do care about every student doing well. They will give you help when you need it and have lots of ways to make sure you don't fall behind. You did well in your last school and you like school, so we have no reason to think that you won't do well here."

"I know, Mom," he answered, with that I've-heard-this-before tone. She knew he was still worried, and in a sense, she was too.

Eva Taylor was surprised to feel the butterflies in her stomach. This was the start of her twelfth year as a middle school principal and she had taught for ten years before that. Everything was ready for opening day. The building looked great. All of the teachers had their rooms ready. The secretaries, the nurses, the teaching assistants, and even the custodians were excited and ready to begin the year.

Mrs. Taylor considered herself fortunate to work in the Blue Fields School District. Compared with her former district, Blue Fields was a breath of fresh air. In her nine years at Blue Fields, Mrs. Taylor had learned quite a bit about continuous improvement, the model adapted from the business world that they used to run their district. As one of the more senior administrators, she had helped the district implement the model from its early stages and experienced the benefits directly.

So, the district was fine, the building was shining, and the staff were all in place and ready to go . . . why the butterflies? What was even more perplexing to Eva was that she had never felt more prepared for an opening day. Over the years, she had come to learn that getting a school ready is much more than having fresh paint, clean floors, competent staff, and the latest computers. The real focus at Blue Fields was on the students. What will they need to have a great year? More importantly, how does this year fit into all of the others in their K–12 experience? What will we need to do for the sixth, seventh, and eighth graders so that they will graduate at their highest potential in seven years, six years, or five years?

Mrs. Taylor knew that all of these questions addressed category three of the Baldrige criteria, a well-known and highly reputable set of standards for the continuous-improvement model. Baldrige has seven categories in all. Category three is student and stakeholder focus. This is where organizations take the time to define their primary customers and the other important groups of people they serve—their stakeholders.

Once an organization knows whom it serves, it must then find out what it is that they need. When she first heard this concept, Mrs. Taylor thought, "Well, isn't this a little too obvious? Our customers obviously are our students and what they need, obviously, is a good education."

But she came to learn it is much more complex. What does a good education mean? More importantly, what does it mean for *our* students? What do they and their families want for them upon graduation? What are the cultural priorities? What is important to *them*? And, how do you get the answers to these questions?

Learning about the needs of your customers is critical for business success. If you don't satisfy their needs, they will take their business someplace else. The same is somewhat true for education. Families with the resources can opt for a private school if they are not satisfied with the public schools. Charter schools and vouchers also provide options. More and more, schools are learning that they need to be better listeners if they want to retain their students.

Since first learning about continuous improvement, the administration at Blue Fields worked on their listening. They began using surveys and focus groups to find out what people liked and didn't like, and why. In one survey, the students reported dissatisfaction with the food in the cafeteria. Mrs. Taylor brought together a group of student leaders and the cafeteria manager. They conducted an additional survey to find out exactly what the students liked and did not like and asked for their ideas for new menu items.

Blue Fields also began looking at utilization data. They looked at how many students took French vs. Latin and how many signed up for lacrosse vs. softball. They started advisory committees for programs such as adult education and professional development and considering when they needed to build a new school. The people on these committees had real input and a direct line to the administration.

The more listening the administration did, the less surprises they had. Without realizing it, they had also fostered an environment where students, parents, staff, and community members could voice their opinions before they became problems. Sure, they still had problems, but nowhere near what they used to have. Unlike their neighboring school district, most of the Blue Fields board of education meetings followed the agenda with little criticism from the audience.

This listening and learning carried over into the classrooms as well. Mrs. Taylor and her teachers knew about the learning needs of each and every student coming into her building that morning. The teachers received data on each of the students in their class. This provided the teachers and the district with enough time to put into place any new resources they would need to meet the needs of this next class.

Mrs. Taylor also had a good handle on the expectations of her students' parents. From the parent surveys, active participation of the PTA, and structured dialogues with groups of parents throughout the school year, she knew what was important to them. She was anxious for them to see the visitors table just inside the front door this year, a response to their concerns last year about security in the building. She was also looking forward to the first dialogue with the seventh grade parents in which they were going to discuss the new homework policy and what they could expect in the way of changes from last year's homework in the sixth grade.

But that was in two weeks and the students were about to arrive. With all that she had to think about, Bill was amazed that she took the time to check in with him. This was his first day as an eighth-grade math teacher at Blue Fields Middle School. He was one of three new teachers in the building this year and she made it a point to see each one of them personally on that very busy morning.

"Good morning, William," she said, with a big smile on her face. "How are you doing? All ready?"

Although he was nervous, Bill had never felt more ready on the first day of school, and here he was in an entirely new job in an entirely new district. But Blue Fields had a very different approach to teacher preparation than he had experienced in his other school. Throughout the interview process, they made the expectations very clear. They talked about the district's goals and how they use data to measure their progress toward those goals. During the new-teacher orientation, they got a better understanding of the district's philosophy and culture and they saw examples of how they would learn to use the continuous-improvement model in their classrooms.

"Actually, I feel great," he responded. "Thanks for asking and thanks for helping me to prepare." Unlike other districts, all teachers at Blue Fields receive detailed student assessment data on each student. Bill knew how they had done the previous year, as well as in the fifth and sixth grades, before coming to him, and any highlights from their elementary years. He already had a sense of which students were going to need additional support but knew that he had to conduct his own preassessment tests during these first two weeks.

"You're welcome," Mrs. Taylor answered. "I'll check back with you later in the day, but if you need me for anything, don't hesitate to ask," she said and scurried off to her next checkpoint.

It wasn't until four days later that Bill asked to see her. The opening had gone well. He liked his schedule and the kids were great. He did have a concern about one student, Malcolm, who had transferred in from another district. Since this student was new to the system, Bill did not have the same assessment data for Malcolm as he did for the other students and he couldn't go down the hall to speak with Malcolm's teachers from last year.

In the meeting, Bill shared his concerns about Malcolm with Mrs. Taylor. "I see a real gap between his current understanding and the materials we are presenting," he explained.

"How do you know that it's his level of understanding and not a reaction to being a new kid in a new school?" she challenged him. Fortunately, he had administered the preassessment test to Malcolm and it showed glaring deficiencies in some areas.

"On the preassessment, he scored very low in four of the six areas," Bill answered and showed her the results. "Could it be that the seventh grade curriculum in his last school was different than ours?"

"That is entirely possible," she answered. "How do you think we should address this?"

"Why don't I spend a little extra time with him over the next few days to get a better handle on whether he actually has been introduced to these concepts. If he has, then we may be able to catch him up with some extra help. If it is more serious, we may need to consider the math academic lab or even a course change," Bill answered.

Evidently, it was the right answer. Mrs. Taylor beamed and said, "Good suggestions, William, I think you are going to do very well here in Blue Fields. Keep me posted, okay?"

Essential Question: Why Start in the Middle?

The Baldrige criteria for education comprises seven categories.

Category 1: Leadership
Category 2: Planning
Category 3: Student and stakeholder needs
Category 4: Data analysis
Category 5: Faculty and staff focus
Category 6: Process management
Category 7: Results

Each of the first six categories covers a vital component of the district's operations. Category 7, results, is where districts report their measured progress for categories 1 through 6.

Typically, the tendency is to begin at the beginning, in this case, leadership. However, in order to maximize a leadership system, schools and districts need to know about their customers—their students. They also need to know about their stakeholders. Stakeholders could include faculty and staff, parents, local community members, higher education, local businesses, feeder schools, and other segments in the community that have a vested interest in the schools. They could also include volunteers and business partners, basically any groups whose support you rely upon to serve your students.

Category 3 focuses on how schools define and learn about the needs of their students and their stakeholders. Typical methods include surveys and focus groups. The Blue Fields district conducts a comprehensive satisfaction survey with its students, parents, and staff every three years. In between the comprehensive survey, they administer smaller dip-stick assessments—similar to checking the oil level in a car's engine; they check if they are making progress or if any new problems have cropped up. They also survey their alumni every three years, asking them how well the district prepared them for college and beyond.

Category 3 also concerns the processes organizations use to understand the priorities of their customers. Processes are organized, systematic methods for accomplishing tasks—they are not one-shot deals. A solid continuous-improvement process includes four steps—plan, do, study, act—and provides ongoing mechanisms for schools to evaluate and improve their systems.

The difference between a school using continuous improvement and one that is not can be seen in how the school responds to student needs. Let's say two districts learn that there are new standards being imposed by their state education department in reading and writing in grades one through three. District A checks with other districts in a neighboring state who went through a similar challenge two years ago. They learn about a curriculum package that specializes in supporting students for most of these new standards. They purchase the package, train the teachers, and hope for the best. When the students fail to meet the new standards, they abandon the package and look for a new one.

District B, however, has a process they follow whenever a new student need is presented. They first conduct a thorough analysis of the need. In this case, they break down the new standards and develop a crosswalk delineating what is new vs. what is aligned with what they are already teaching (step one: plan). They rewrite their curriculum maps to include the new material. They purchase whatever new resources they need, again after a thorough, objective analysis. They train the teachers in the new curriculum and in any new instructional strategies they may need (step two: do). They develop interim assessments whereby teachers can check for understanding throughout the school year. They conduct gap analyses when students miss material on the interim assessments and then adjust their curriculum or instruction accordingly. Not surprisingly, the students do well on the standardized assessments. They further analyze student performance by teacher (step three: study). They identify best practices, adopt those as standard practices, and train other teachers in them (step four: act).

Continuous-improvement school districts, such as Blue Fields, use this same plan-do-study-act template for all of their student and stakeholder needs. Not only do they consider the needs of the students currently enrolled in their schools, they also anticipate the needs of their future customers. Through the years, Eva Taylor has learned that student needs come first. She has seen many instances where districts put elaborate, flashy programs in place without doing their homework. They hire new program leaders, reassign and retrain staff, and purchase fancy stuff, only to miss the mark.

As Mrs. Taylor has learned through her superintendent, Dr. Johnston, you need to start with research, determine your needs, and then deploy your resources. And that includes leadership. For example, if you have a strong interest among your students and families in theater and music, your leadership team needs to have knowledge and expertise in that area. If many of your families are second- and third-generation tradespeople (carpenters, plumbers, electricians) and have those expectations for their children, your program should integrate technical training with college preparatory.

Quality organizations also learn the value of complaints. Complaints provide insight into satisfaction—both satisfaction levels and areas of satisfaction. Schools committed to continuous improvement have a process in place to respond to complaints and use the data they collect on complaints to improve their service to students.

In his short time at Blue Fields, Bill has already learned the valuable lesson of assessing his customer's needs. He realizes that if he had gone in to Mrs. Taylor without the preassessment test data, she would have sent him back. Because he had done the research, he was now better positioned to help Malcolm in a more efficient and proactive way.

Student needs come first. Start with category three. Start in the middle.

3

THE BOSS GOES FIRST: MODEL THE PROCESS

LEADERSHIP

Bill had been teaching eighth-grade math at the middle school for about six weeks now and already he knew he was in a different kind of organization. During his planning conference with Mrs. Taylor, he became aware of what the district refers to as "key performance measures." Specifically, these measures set the performance goal for key indicators by title and current rate of performance. He had already scanned the list and to his panic he saw the words "eighth grade." He knew he was on the line for some kind of measure. He had hoped that by being in the middle school the performance measures would miss him or that the district did not count middle school measures.

Bill recalled the conference with the principal as he drove home that afternoon.

"If you notice," Mrs. Taylor had said, "the district has set math goals for the eighth grade. As one of teachers you need to be aware of the goals and the current level of performance. Last year 91 percent of our students passed the rigorous new math exam for the state. We want to raise this score. I guess the words I am searching for is that we want to help you in your efforts to raise this rate."

Bill's mind was racing. This was his first evaluation-type meeting with the principal. He knew his teaching was off to a good start. The students liked him, his peers had accepted him even though he was a beginning teacher, and he had had a few parent meetings, which went well. Students' grades were above average on the short quizzes he had given. Most of the students were doing well. There were a few, particularly the new student, Malcolm, who were having trouble, but Bill felt these few would not be held against him. But now, here was this principal telling him to raise the bar, sort of.

"My students seem to be doing well. The classes have grades in the 80s and 90s and most of the homework is turned in on time. Parents are pleased, at least the ones I have talked with," Bill said in his defense. "Malcolm, the boy I spoke to you about in the first few days, is still failing some of the quizzes," he admitted.

"Well, most of what you tell me is a good sign, Bill," said Mrs. Taylor. "I am sure that you are happy that the year has started off well. Malcolm's needs have to be addressed. You need to be aware, Bill, that the district, I and the other members of the math department, in particular, have set these goals. Yes, we are raising the number of students passing each year. We fully expect 100 percent of our eighth graders will pass this exam in three years. Each year we move closer. I will expect you to report on student achievement each quarter, as I track these goals quarterly. I want these goals to become yours, Bill."

Bill felt the pressure. He looked again at the long list of what was called "Leadership Performance Review." He focused on his segment and he now saw the organization of what the principal had said.

"Bill, I was not giving lip service to the fact that we will help you meet this goal," said Mrs. Taylor.

Bill was wondering about that line. He knew all bosses had to say that. He knew he'd be the one in the fire (so long, tenure!) if he did not produce. Anyway, he thought, let her continue.

"You know our mission is that *Every Child Can and Will Learn*. That is what is behind these performance goals," she said. "We really believe that 100 percent of our kids can get there. You need to believe that too, Bill. It is not going to work if only I believe it. You need to believe it as well. We all need to believe it. It is the vision thing.

"Let me give you a short explanation of what I am talking about. A few years ago we did a survey of parents in the district. We asked them all sorts of questions about a variety of items affecting school life. We also asked the staff a number of similar but building-related questions. We also surveyed students present and past, our alumni. We do this about every three years and on a smaller scale every year. Our communications director tells me it is a real challenge to collect, disaggregate, and analyze these every year. But we do get good information.

"An item reported as low in satisfaction among parents in our middle school and in our high school was the quality of math instruction at the middle school. I did not know what this rating meant at the time, and frankly, I was shocked. I thought we were doing a great job. At the time we had one of the highest passing rates in the county on the state exams. But our parents were telling us something different. They did not believe it!

"I thought the superintendent, Dr. Johnston, was going to fry me in oil. Well, maybe not oil but certainly water."

Bill is thinking that this will probably be his fate if he does not meet the performance goals.

"You know, Bill, he did not. In fact he came over for my performance review and said he would help me. He did not give me lip service either. He helped me gather resources to map the curriculum, analyze the gap, and provide staff development, particularly in teaching students to use hands-on manipulatives to learn equations, and reminded me to keep focus on instruction."

Bill thought that he had better remember these terms "map the curriculum, analyze the gap." What gap, anyway? He remembered that Dr. Johnston had discussed staff development during his interview. It had seemed to be lip service to Bill. Apparently it was not. Bill thought he had better sign up for that staff development as soon as possible. And what about teaching equations using hands-on manipulatives? How do you teach *that*? he thought.

Mrs. Taylor continued, "On top of that, we heard from our students that middle school math was boring. Well, they didn't use that term but low satisfaction meant the same thing.

"I point out these survey results, Bill, because they provide a background for why we developed performance goals for eighth-grade math. Our parents and students were telling us that we had a problem. It was not the kids' fault. We could not say, 'Well, I taught it, they just didn't learn it.' In fact, we did not teach it. It was a hard fact to face."

"You mean that all the district goals are formulated on information received in surveys?" Bill asked.

"Surveys and other listening posts in our community, such as leadership membership on the PTA leadership council, Rotary, and Chamber of

Commerce. Stakeholder input, together with review of past performance results and future needs, are very important to us, Bill," said Mrs. Taylor. "Faculty is included in this input. We did not go wild in responding to these survey results. I was careful to involve the middle school staff in formulating the performance goals as a response. The central office did not come down here and yell at us. They knew as we did that the survey results had to be addressed. They listened first to the response from our building—from the staff. Then they asked how they could help. Yes, they added direction and did tell us to move more quickly in some areas, but in essence they helped us build capacity at our building level so we could respond."

"I see," Bill said. Thinking that perhaps it was safe to say something, he asked if he could be involved in a committee working on the problem. Bill was not sure what that would consist of, but clearly from Mrs. Taylor's statements, faculty were seen as important in addressing the needs of the students. Bill felt important in this task, though he was unsure. Certainly Mrs. Taylor gave him the lead and sense that his input was important.

"Excellent, yes, we need your involvement," she said. "I have to rely on my faculty to make the decisions to reach these goals. I know instruction, Bill, but I don't know how to teach math as well as some of the veteran teachers in this building. You need to learn from them. I believe in my staff and that they can reach the 100 percent goal. That is what our parents want. Our students want more active learning with relevancy. Our staff, we know from surveys, want to be prized and valued."

"So you know you have reached your goal when 100 percent have passed the state math exam and the survey results improve?" Bill asked.

"Yes, continuous improvement is built on the idea that we get better each year. We set our goals based on customer needs, determined in this case by student exam results and survey results. We build the capacity to reach these goals. It is all about you believing in you. In my case it is about believing my staff can do it. Also, I also know that Dr. Johnston believes that I can reach our goals."

Bill knew at this point he had to find a way to help Malcolm and the other students achieve more. It was not because Mrs. Taylor told him that he had to but, rather, after this meeting he felt he could.

As Bill turned into his driveway he mentally summed up the meeting, coming to the understanding that Mrs. Taylor and the other district staff he knew really believed in this "all kids can learn" stuff. The poster outside Dr. Johnston's office and the small bookmark he gave him during the interview had mission, goals, and value statements that people here in Blue Fields actually believed. They even charted how to fulfill them. Now here I am, Bill said to himself, believing the stuff as well.

Essential Question: Why Does the Boss Go First?

Most staff reading the title to this chapter would frown at such a statement. Could any organization be as pompous as to actually state that? Well, in fact, no matter how talented and experienced a staff may be, if the boss does not believe in and model the district commitment to continuous improvement, there is no way any district mission, statement, or values will ever be fulfilled. Simply put, if the leader does not believe, the staff will not.

Recall the conference between Bill and Mrs. Taylor. The principal showed leadership from the start. She clearly and repeatedly told Bill that she believed in him and believed in the ability of all her students to learn. High expectations were set from the beginning and Bill never felt they were false. She detailed her vision and explained how she became to believe in the process as well. She modeled for Bill how to think through the process of believing in the vision that all students can learn. In the beginning, Bill was full of doubt. But as he reflected, he began to gain the sense of what continuous improvement was all about.

You might have noticed that during the conference Mrs. Taylor led Bill through a process that actually helped Bill capture the "vision thing." She demonstrated leadership behavior throughout. First, she held a performance review meeting with Bill early in the school year. In a direct manner she informed him of the building goals, the math department goals, and the goals for his class. Bill had a very clear picture from the beginning that instruction and learning were at the core of the district continuous-improvement plan.

Mrs. Taylor then helped Bill internalize these goals by sharing with him her own journey in understanding continuous improvement. She talked about her own self-doubts and fear of being punished if test scores did not get better. She was telling Bill that the district is not about checking if teachers or even principals are doing wrong but about helping them become better teachers and principals.

Next she told Bill that solving student achievement problems was a collaborative effort. She expected staff to support each other and work as a team to achieve the goals. Her management style, as reflected in the superintendent's style, was not top down. It was not even bottom up. It was a management style of collaboration, respect, and a clear focus on continuous improvement. Staff felt valued and this level of satisfaction was so important that it was measured in a survey each year.

The principal recognized that Bill, as a beginning teacher in this district, was not professionally ready to assume responsibility for making building-level decisions. Bill was eager to join a working committee because he sensed they were valued. But she told him that as part of her leadership style she believed in delegation. She mentioned how senior staff members were involved in helping to make decisions that affected the building. She did tell Bill that he was responsible for his small piece of the building. That is, it was his responsibility to find a way so that all children, including Malcolm, could achieve.

As Bill arrived home, he felt that he had a firm grasp of what the district mission and values were. He knew how they become operational in his own classroom and how the process of continuous improvement was the key to fulfilling the mission. While at the beginning of the day he had been satisfied with his own students' achievement as a group, by the end of the day he knew he had more work to accomplish. He set out to help Malcolm and the other students achieve.

At the same time, Bill developed a new appreciation for how Mrs. Taylor and Dr. Johnston really did practice what they preached. Granted, he was not aware of how involved they and the other senior leaders were in developing and improving their management system. But it was clearly evident that they knew what they were doing.

For example, one of the key responsibilities of district and building leadership was to maintain and report on their commitment to key practices relating to regulatory, legal, and ethical standards. These were national, state, local, or district policies that needed to be maintained. Figure 3.1 shows a sample chart for organizing such key practices.

Evaluating performance is another key function of management. Baldrige asks districts to define their process for doing so. Typically, this is a consistent and comprehensive system based on data. It should allow

	Key Practices	*Measures*	*Targets*
Regulatory	Right to Know	# of complaints	0
	OSHA	# of violations	0
	State Education Dept.	Record of compliance	100%
	IDEA (Disabilities Act)	Rate of compliance	100%
	Health/Safety Committee	Potential # of alerts	0
Legal	Sexual Harassment	Complaints	0
	Policy Book	Lawsuits	0
	Contracts	Grievances	0
	Fire Inspections	Infractions noted to SED	0
Ethical	Board Code of Ethics	# of violations	0
	Staff Code of Ethics	# of violations	0
	Student Code of Conduct	# of violations	0
	Athlete Code of Conduct	# of violations	0

Note: OSHA = Office of Safety and Health Administration; IDEA = Individuals with Disabilities in Education Act; SED = State Education Department.

Figure 3.1. Key Practices, Measures, and Targets

for leaders to adapt the organization's operations when warranted, either by adjusting minimum expectations (baselines) or by deploying new practices or setting new standards based on positive results. An example of such a process is shown in figure 3.2.

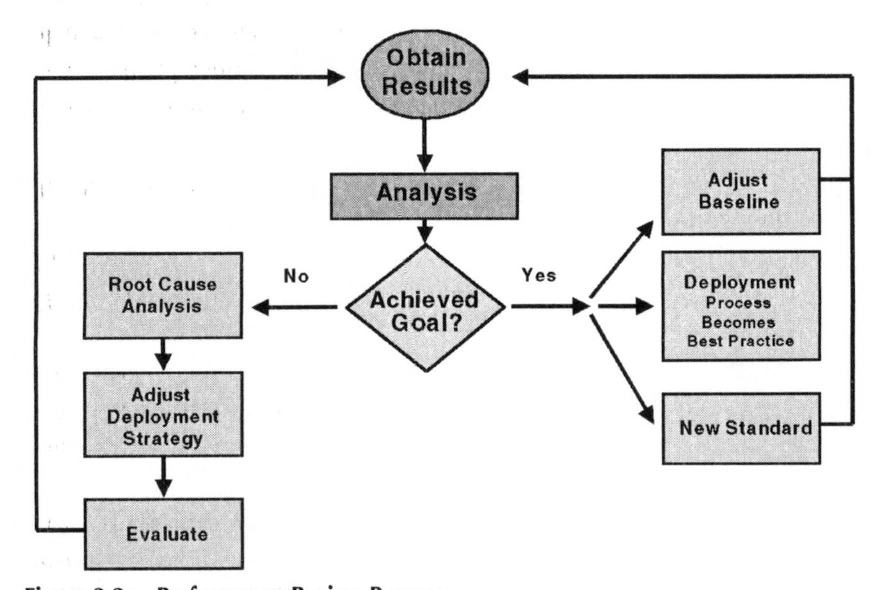

Figure 3.2. Performance Review Process

4

A PLAN FOR ME: CHART THE COURSE

STRATEGIC PLANNING

"Why was the Blue Fields School District so much better?" Jeannie's friend asked.

Jeannie wasn't sure. "Well, Malcolm's been there now for almost half the year. I'm aware of some things they do differently in comparison with his old school, but I'm not sure if this is why they are so much better," she said.

"One thing I can tell you is that they are far more diagnostic in their teaching, always checking to see if their students are progressing. If a student is struggling, then the teacher adapts his instruction or offers extra help or some other support. Just look at Malcolm and how they've handled his struggle with math," she continued.

She also knew that they took more interest in the needs of their students and their families. Jeannie felt more involved and more informed than she had in their former district. Parents had a real voice in important matters, such as hiring staff and reviewing proposed policies and being asked their opinions in surveys and focus groups and meetings. Students were involved, too.

"It also seems that the morale among the staff is better," Jeanne said to her friend. "They just seem happier at their work. They really like their students and seem to be better prepared than the teachers Malcolm had before," she said, as she thought more about it.

But she honestly could not tell her friend why this was all different. She knew that Blue Fields had won the Baldrige award, but did not know enough about it to understand how it made a difference. In fact, in many ways, walking through the Blue Fields schools was the same as walking through most other schools. Students were sitting at desks or computers or in gym or art or music classes. Teachers were teaching. Administrators were in their offices or in meetings or in hallways. The board of education held regular meetings—all very much the same as other districts.

What was not apparent to Jeannie was the planning that went on behind all of these activities. Very little that happened at Blue Fields happened by chance. Instruction was planned. New programs were planned. Budgets were planned.

Certainly, or at least hopefully, all school districts plan in some way or another. They don't just open buildings, hire teachers, buy supplies, and start school.

What the administration at Blue Fields learned through the Baldrige process was how to align everyone's activities according to the needs of the students. They learned how to think in long-term and short-term capacities and how plans are made based on information and data, not because they are "good ideas" or "worked great" in another district.

Blue Fields plans at three levels—the district level, the building level, and the classroom level. Within two weeks after the end of every school year, Dr. Johnston conducts an administrative retreat for all of the district administrators. They take two days to review their performance on all of the long-term (which they call "lag") goals and short-term (called "lead") goals they had set for themselves the summer before. They look at national research and their own survey results to determine what new needs their students and families have. They analyze new standards and requirements from places such as the state education department, federal agencies, and colleges and universities. They have very open and frank discussions about which directions they should consider for the coming year.

Approximately six weeks later, they come together again for their administrative advance. They review any new data that their assistant superintendent has since collected. They look at last year's lag and lead goals, which are organized under the district's three strategic goals (academics, perception, and fiscal stability), to see if they need to be changed. Sometimes new mandates require that they abandon or change goals. Other times, the goals stay the same, but the measures and targets change. For example, improving elementary students' performance in writing has been a long-standing lead goal. Blue Fields used to use the DOG tests to measure their progress. For a number of years, between 99 and 100 percent of all of the elementary students were meeting standards on the exam, so Blue Fields abandoned the DOG and adopted the more challenging ABC writing test in its place.

Once they have their lag and lead goals set, the administrators then set target performance levels for each goal. At Blue Fields, every goal must have a measure—otherwise, how will they know they have reached it? And each measure has a target. For example, under the strategic goal of improving academic performance, one of the lag goals is to increase the number of students who attain the more rigorous state-level high school diploma. The ultimate goal is for a 100 percent regents diploma rate. Last year 89 percent of the graduating class received a regents diploma, so the target for the following year moves to 91 percent.

So, now they know where they want to be. The next question becomes, How will they get there? What will they need to do in order to reach their new targets? At Blue Fields, the administrators then plan what they call "projects"—these are the actions that they will take during the coming year to improve academic performance, improve the perception of their district, and improve fiscal efficiency. Typically, projects are defined as a year or less in length but can extend into several years with different phases for each year. Each project has an administrator or set of administrators responsible for it. They report to Dr. Johnston quarterly on the project's approach, deployment, and results.

For example, under the strategic goal to improve academic performance, is an annual project to rewrite the math curriculum for grades five, six, and seven. The project's aim is to increase the percentage of eighth graders who meet the standard on the state math exam. This is because fourth graders performed well on the state exams, but eighth graders did not. Analysis of the test results showed consistent gaps across certain units suggesting weak curriculum. The director of curriculum worked with math teachers in grade-level teams to rewrite the curriculum.

Before goals and projects are adopted, Dr. Johnston presents them to the board of education. Board members provide input into the plan, seek clarification, and approve the plan each year. They call this planning structure the Golden Thread. An example is shown in figure 4.1.

In September of each year, once the district's lag and lead goals and targets are established and projects outlined, the school-building principals then take the strategic plan to their building leadership teams. Building leadership teams are shared decision-making teams comprising teachers, staff, and parents for each building. The high school team also includes student representatives. Each building team reviews the district plan and develops an annual building plan with projects specific to their building for the year. All building projects must support the district strategic goals. As with the district plan, the board of education also provides input into and approves the building plans.

For example, one of the projects Eva Taylor had for last year was to institute a disciplinary program for middle school students' behavior on the school bus. The district had received numerous complaints from parents about the middle school buses, and this was reflected on the parent-satisfaction survey. Mrs. Taylor worked with her teaching assistants and the district's transportation supervisor to develop a discipline and reporting system. She also reviewed the proposed system with her PTA. They implemented the system and monitored results. Behavior improved and the number of complaints decreased.

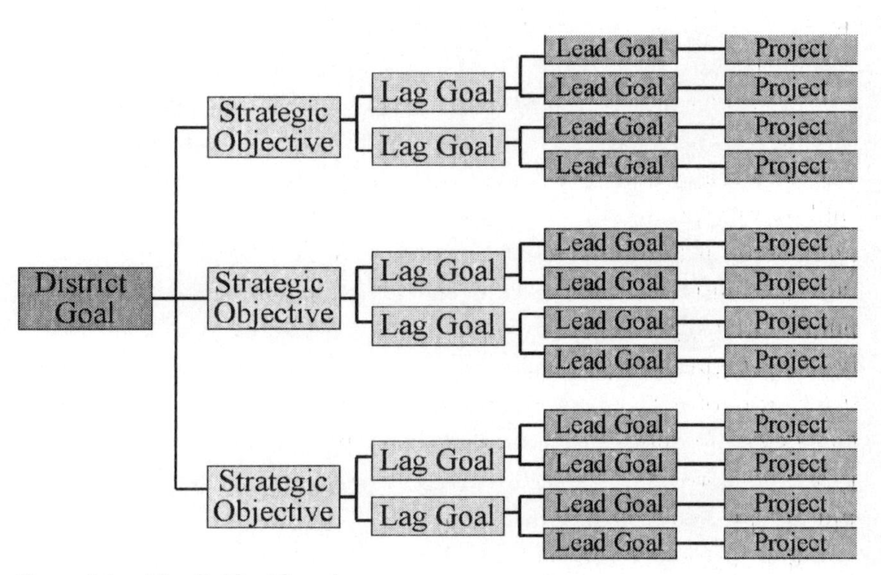

Figure 4.1. The Golden Thread

Other districts have bus discipline programs. The difference with the Blue Fields program is that it is linked to the district's strategic plan. Everyone working on the bus-behavior problem knows that the ultimate goal here is to improve student safety, thereby increasing parent satisfaction and improving how the district is perceived. Perception is very important at Blue Fields. Each year, district residents vote on the school budget. Blue Fields has enjoyed a three-to-one positive-to-negative vote ratio for more than ten years. This positive climate not only provides funding for district programs, it spills over into other areas of community support on which the district relies.

Teachers at Blue Fields also plan for the learning that happens in their classrooms. At the beginning of each year, every teacher meets with the building principal to review his or her individual goals and objectives. This personalized plan is based on the teacher's past performance, the needs of the students (all researched and based on data), and the teacher's personal career goals. Together, they develop an annual plan of how the teacher will meet the new targets for the students. This plan can include integrating new teaching strategies, changing grading or assessment techniques, being assigned a mentor, or participating in professional development programs such as workshops, in-service training courses, and conferences.

Teachers at Blue Fields use the A+ Approach for Classroom Instruction, a process they have developed that follows the plan-do-study-act model of improvement. In the plan phase, teachers analyze the needs of their students. They do this in a wide variety of ways. Obviously, they use assessment data such as test scores and lab grades and homework grades. Blue Fields administrators teach the faculty how to use the data to improve their instruction. They learn to look for trends and for gaps to see if individual students are struggling or if the entire class or segments within the class are not meeting the standard.

Teachers also use softer assessments. They consider whether a student has something occurring in his or her personal life that may be interfering with academics. They also rely on educational research and research on children and learning. Armed with all of this information and analysis, they then plan the learning that will occur in their classroom by aligning their curriculum (what they teach) and their instruction (how they teach), all based on the needs of their students.

For example, Bill used a preassessment test to find Malcolm's difficulties in mathematics. Understanding that Malcolm had just arrived at Blue Fields from another district, Bill confirmed that Malcolm either had not been introduced to some of the subject matter or had been introduced to it but had not mastered it. Bill's goal for Malcolm was to bring him up to the level of the other students in his class. Therefore, Bill prescribed extra support through an additional period of math each day in the math lab in his school. Bill will work individually with Malcolm after school and during his lunch to close the gap.

While Jeannie can understand how this process relates to her son, she does not necessarily see it in the context of the bigger picture. The layers of planning that occur behind helping Malcolm master mathematics are somewhat transparent to students and families. But it is absolutely essential to the success at Blue Fields. Chart your course.

Essential Question: If You Don't Know Where You Are Going, How Will You Know When You've Gotten There?

All organizations need direction. Effective organizations have direction that is based on strategic thinking and action. Strategic thinking must be based on the researched needs of the customers you are serving if your organization is going to meet those needs. For schools, our primary customers are our students and our service is teaching and learning. All planning must focus on or somehow support instruction.

After delineating the key requirements of students and other stakeholders in your district (parents, taxpayers, faculty and staff, higher education, etc.), school leaders in Baldrige organizations use a strategic planning process to align all of the work activities to meet those requirements. This involves both short-term and long-term thinking. What do we need to do today, next week, next month, and next year in order to accomplish our goals?

Because requirements sometimes change, schools must also maintain flexibility to adapt and switch in their planning. For example, new legislation may come down from the state education department in the middle of the school year reducing the amount of state aid coming to your district. How will you adapt to still meet the needs of your students with reduced resources? You may consider redeploying faculty and staff, reorganizing programs, or seeking alternative funding as possible solutions.

Responding to current needs is only part of a strategic planning process. Refined organizations have systems in place to prepare for future needs as well. What will the students arriving in your district in 2005 need to know to be successful upon graduation in 2018? How will outside influences—such as technology, the economy, demographics, and the workforce—affect your school district during this time frame?

Knowing how you will measure your progress is an integral part of strategic planning. Based on the needs, what are your goals? Each goal needs a measure. If you can't measure it, then how will you know you have accomplished it?

Charting the course for your organization provides a blueprint for direction. Everyone in your organization needs to know where you are headed—"What is the goal?"—and how you will get there—"What are we doing?" If an action is taking place that does not support your direction, then why are you doing it?

An effective planning process can be both rigid and fluid at the same time: rigid in how you assess needs, align actions, and measure results and fluid in being positioned to alter your plan as needs or results dictate.

Take the time to chart your course. Find out what your students and families and taxpayers want and need. Know what they require. Help everyone in your organization to understand these needs. Organize your activities around meeting them. Measure your progress and celebrate your success. When you've reached your goal, set a higher one and make a new plan.

5

IN GOD WE TRUST: ALL OTHERS BRING DATA

INFORMATION AND ANALYSIS

It was the second Tuesday of the month—faculty meeting day. Bill found himself thinking about how much he used to dread faculty meetings in his last district. They were so boring—usually just a string of announcements full of deadlines, policies, requirements, and cautions. So far, this was not the case at Blue Fields Middle School. Sure, there were the announcements, but that wasn't the whole focus. Mrs. Taylor used this time to really talk with the faculty about much more important things—how the kids were doing, how the staff was doing, where the district was headed, and why.

By now, Bill had been to three faculty meetings—and they were all pretty interesting. In addition to Mrs. Taylor's discussions, sometimes teachers gave presentations. Usually, it was on something fairly unusual they were doing. Always, there was a connection between the activity and the outcome. Mrs. Taylor also presented a lot of results and data. During the September meeting, she reviewed the school's performance for the prior school year. She showed where the students had done well and where they did not do so well. She then presented the building's goals for the coming year.

Bill found a seat near the other math teachers. He loved how everyone was laughing and joking. They just seemed to really like being there, and he did, too. Mrs. Taylor began the meeting. The first item on the agenda was "Alumni Survey." Bill was curious.

Evidently, every three years, Blue Fields does a survey of their alumni. The survey asks very pointed questions about how well prepared the alumni felt they were for college and beyond. What a great idea, Bill thought. In his former district, they would probably be afraid to ask those questions for fear of the answers they would get.

As Mrs. Taylor went through the results of the survey, Bill saw the many things that Blue Fields was doing right. Alumni said they felt very well prepared in math and science and computers. Mrs. Taylor reminded them that this is a reflection on all of them, not just the high school staff, and everyone clapped. Then, Mrs. Taylor showed them the areas where the alumni reported less satisfaction. They said that they had not read as many books as some of their fellow college students and that they felt less prepared to do public speaking.

Right away, teachers started to offer possible solutions to the problem—require more reading, increase library time, add a speech class. Mrs. Taylor explained that the district administration was already considering many of these things and that the building team would be working on specific approaches for the middle school. Bill found himself thinking about how he could offer more opportunities for his students to speak in front of their peers during his math class—perhaps explaining a formula or reading a word problem.

A few of the more veteran teachers offered their opinions, and then Mrs. Taylor moved on to the announcements. Bill couldn't keep his mind from drifting back to the alumni—how cool it was that the district knew it had deficiencies and how important it was to fix them. Again, he found himself thinking about his former district and how, if they actually had taken the time to ask the alumni, they would probably just come up with a whole list of excuses why the alumni were not satisfied and probably blame their parents for not reading to them enough.

After only a few short months, Bill knew that the crux of the issue was actually getting the data. It didn't take long for him to see the pattern—everything they did at Blue Fields was based around data. Dr. Johnston had talked about it in his interview, but Bill didn't really understand it at the time. Little by little, it was becoming much more clear.

During the two superintendent conference days, Dr. Johnston shared data with the entire staff. He flashed test score numbers and graduation rates and tax rates in a slide presentation. He showed how the male students compared with the female students, how the science grades compared with the foreign language grades, and even how the special ed kids did—Bill thought that was pretty gutsy.

Dr. Johnston then told them about how the board of education had approved the district goals for the coming year. Each goal had a measure—such as 60 percent mastery on the state biology exam or 95 percent parent satisfaction with district communications. Again, Bill thought this was pretty gutsy. But at the same time, he liked seeing the big picture and where he fit.

Where he fit was never more obvious to him than when he met with Mrs. Taylor after the first quarter. During the meeting, she produced a printout of all of Bill's students, by class, and their quarter grades. Evidently, the district uses an electronic data warehouse to store and organize student data. They can manipulate this information in an endless number of ways, rather easily, to help them understand both student and teacher performance.

Mrs. Taylor shared with Bill how she looks at the grades by section, to see if his fourth-period class is doing any better or worse than his seventh-period class. She also showed him how the other eighth-grade math classes were doing, including not only the average for the whole grade but breakouts by period and individual students. Mrs. Taylor looked at the percentage of Bill's students who achieved mastery (85 percent or higher) and those who were failing and then compared that with the same percentages for the other eighth-grade math teachers.

For the most part, Bill's students' were performing similarly to the other eighth graders. She asked him about the assessments he used in class—how he grades homework and quizzes. They talked about how he uses these assessments to inform his teaching—exactly the same approach he was learning in his new-teacher class taught by the assistant superintendent. Evidently, all of these administrators talk to one another, he thought.

Mrs. Taylor also spent quite a bit of time on the students who were failing. She asked Bill why they were not performing to standard and what plans he had to support them. Bill couldn't help but think about Dr. Johnston and the district mission—while the data showed that some kids weren't cutting it, that clearly was not acceptable because Every Child Can and Will Learn. It was up to Bill to make it happen. And, thankfully, he had help.

Bill talked about the two students who he knew had the potential to pass but not the drive. While they grasped concepts easily, they had poor attendance and homework records and bad attitudes and were disruptive in class. Mrs. Taylor referred to them as the "third quartile"—not classified as special education, but clearly not meeting standard. She challenged Bill to think about ways to engage them at their level, as well as discussing possible solutions with their guidance counselor, school psychologist, school resource officer, and other support personnel.

Mrs. Taylor also asked Bill about the one special-education student who was mainstreamed into his fourth-period class. The assessment data she had showed that perhaps this was not the best placement for her. Bill explained that the student was definitely challenged in the class, but that he believed she had the potential to pass with some extra support. They talked about options for her and how Bill could track what worked and what did not.

Then the conversation turned to Malcolm. Mrs. Taylor was well aware of the gaps between seventh grade at Malcolm's prior school and Blue Fields' eighth grade. "Eighth grade is extremely important, William," said Mrs. Taylor. "Malcolm needs to master this if he is to have any chance in high school mathematics."

This caught Bill slightly off guard. He was not thinking about Malcolm's experience beyond his class. He was so consumed with getting him caught up in his class. Talk about seeing where you fit into the big picture, he thought. They went on to discuss Malcolm's performance in the math lab and whether Bill had seen any improvements in the in-class assessments. Bill told Mrs. Taylor how he was learning to diagnostically use the feedback from the quizzes and homework and unit tests to help him pinpoint where Malcolm needed help. It was clearly with hands-on equations.

Eva Taylor was pleased. She was pleased with her selection of Bill in hiring and she was pleased with how he was fitting into the district's approaches and philosophy. This thought reminded her of other new teachers who had had to make adjustments. A few years back, they had hired a science teacher who appeared to have the right stuff. For the first three quarters, her students' performance was right on par with the other science teachers. Then came the state science test where her students' average grade was 11 percent lower. This perplexed Eva because, from what she observed, the teacher was a solid teacher. And her in-school assessments showed no major disparity.

In reviewing the results with the teacher, Eva learned that the teacher had built into her grading structure a number of opportunities for extra credit.

Evidently, in her prior teaching experience, she worked with kids who needed to be motivated to perform. This same approach at Blue Fields, however, backfired. Most students took every opportunity for extra credit, thereby inflating their grades and presenting a false picture of their actual performance, which then became evident on the standardized test. By simply uncovering this phenomenon through the data, the teacher changed her grading structure and the gap closed the following year.

Over the years, Eva Taylor had become an expert in her use of data to drive improvement. Thinking back to her earlier years as a principal, and her even earlier years as a teacher, she wondered how she ever made it through those years without it. Data are at the heart of everything they do at Blue Fields. Not in a cold, calculating way but in an open, analytical, informed way. Never is the first reaction to blame someone for bad results. Rather, it is one of grateful discovery as to where problems lie and a targeted approach to coming up with solutions.

Among her peers on the administrative cabinet, Eva is known for her expert use of data. She helps with the data warehouse, making suggestions on how they can improve the system and different ways her peers can use it to help their teachers. Eva also sits on the administration's data subcommittee, the ones to develop the Blue Fields Balanced Scorecard (see figure 5.1) a few years back. They learned about this organizational system for data from the Harvard Business School and found a way to adapt it for education.

In the Blue Fields Balanced Scorecard, there are strategic objectives for each of the district's three overall goals. For each strategic objective, there are lag goals (long-term, summative results) and lead goals (short-term, prescriptive data). The whole idea is that if you improve performance on the lead goals, then the lag goals will also improve. Because it was a relatively new concept for education, Eva and her fellow committee members were continuously analyzing the dynamics between the lag and lead goals.

One of the questions they frequently found themselves asking is whether an individual group of students, known as a cohort, is the reason for a shift in performance. Again, through her research and study of data, Eva learned that improvement or decline cannot be considered a trend after two or three years. You need at least five, and preferably seven, data points to determine a trend. If one class appears to consistently under- or over-perform, this can be accounted for by analyzing trends over time.

Strategic Objectives	*Lag Indicators (long-term)*	*Lead Indicators (predictive)*
	Academic Performance	
Academic Achievement	Regents Diploma Rate	Achievement on 4th and 8th grade state exams CTPIII Reading and Math Achievement Special Education Opportunity
College Admissions	AP Participation Rate AP Performance Rate	Passing Rate on Regents Exams SAT I & II Participation Rate Scholar Athlete Teams
	Perception	
Parent/Community Satisfaction	Market Share	Stakeholder Satisfaction Surveys Adult Education Enrollment Prospective Homeowner Requests New Resident Survey
	Fiscal Stability	
Cost-Effective Fiscal Management	Contain Per-Pupil Expenditure	Reduce Costs in Non-Instructional Areas

Note: CTPIII = Comprehensive Testing Program; SAT = Scholastic Assessment Test; AP = Advanced Placement.

Figure 5.1. The Balanced Scorecard

Another very powerful lesson has been the use of benchmarks. Eva remembered the earlier years when Blue Fields first started to collect and analyze data. Their results looked good, especially when they implemented program changes and saw improvements. Everyone felt great. But, as it turned out, their results were not as good as they could or should have been. Through Baldrige, they learned about benchmark data—finding the best performance or, at the very least, a district that was doing better. Blue Fields did not need to look too far. Suddenly, things did not look so rosy. While it was painfully humbling, it also served as inspiration to do better.

Now, Eva Taylor and her colleagues seek out the highest performers in their state. They want to know if Blue Fields is at the top, and if not, how close they are. This notion of stretching has spilled over to the faculty. Teachers openly talk about "their" students' performance relative to their peers in their department or their grade level and how they are striving for a higher mark next time around.

Eva can't imagine how she would ever do her job without the data. Bill is learning the value of solid information in teaching and learning. What Dr. Johnston said was true, "In God we trust. All others bring data."

Essential Question: Are There Other Measures besides Test Score Data That Can Be Used to Measure Progress at Achieving the District Mission Statement?

There is controversy about the value of scores from standardized tests for data and its relevance in measuring a student's knowledge. So while we want all children to learn, we have to ask ourselves, How do we measure it? In this chapter, Bill used math test score data. Are there other ways to measure student learning?

Most schools are devoted to teaching not only reading and math and other traditional content knowledge but aspects of learning as well. It is important not to rely solely on test score data for a comprehensive assessment of student learning. We also need to know how well schools teach respect, kindness, service toward others, school spirit, and athletics, to name but a few. This kind of knowledge can be measured as well. Here are some examples.

Respect and kindness	Number of suspensions, discipline or bus referrals
Service	Number of community service hours per student
School spirit	The percentage of students involved in clubs, sports, and so on
Athletics	The average grade point average of each team; often referred to as scholar athlete team

It is important that a school community discuss how it can collect data on other aspects of student learning besides achievement test data. Most school communities hold other values as important as grades, and these values should be measured as well.

Districts also need to consider the measures they will use for their support services. This includes both services that directly support students, such as guidance, transportation, and food service, as well as those that indirectly support them but are vital to the functioning of the district, such as personnel, benefits, purchasing, and business-office functions. After determining the key requirements (expectations) for these functions, managers need to identify indicators or measurements for each requirement. Two examples follow:

1. Transportation (busing)
   Key requirement: Students are transported safely
   Indicator: Number of accidents or injuries on the bus
2. Purchasing
   Key requirement: Secure the correct materials in a timely manner
   Indicator: Percentage of orders filled correctly; turnaround time

As with student assessment data, districts need to identify benchmarks for support service measures. However, they need not be limited to other districts or educational organizations. Remember, benchmarks need to represent best in class or, at the very least, a stretch goal. It is entirely possible that an overnight delivery company can serve as a benchmark for a school district's delivery measures or a payroll company can serve as a benchmark for a district's payroll measures.

6

GET OUT THE MAP: UNDERSTANDING THE BLUE FIELDS WAY

PROCESS MANAGEMENT

As Bill was deciding how to help Malcolm he looked over his notes from one of the in-service courses he had taken in the district. He knew he needed to grasp the big picture before he could devise a strategy to improve Malcolm's math grades.

It was the A+ approach that he remembered. It was simple in design (four As) and its name stood for the goal of every school to help students achieve a grade of A+. The approach is really a process map (see figure 6.1) because it reports the educational design and delivery system used at Blue Fields. To a teacher like Bill, it presented an outline of the instructional approaches, modes of teaching, and organizing activities so that he can help Malcolm.

The process map provides sequencing and linkages among the educational programs at Blue Fields. It includes a measurement plan that is holistic and defines what should be measured and how the results should be used. It assumes that faculty at Blue Fields have been trained in how to use it and specifically how to recognize where they are in the process.

The first step, or A, is *Analyze*. Student needs are analyzed by studying the assessment data for gaps in achievement by grade, gender, and cohort as well as by individual student. These may include classroom quizzes, class participation, homework, and project completion. Teachers at Blue Fields are taught and therefore expected to analyze this kind of assessment data regularly. Every quarter the principal reviews the data and reports it to the superintendent. It is

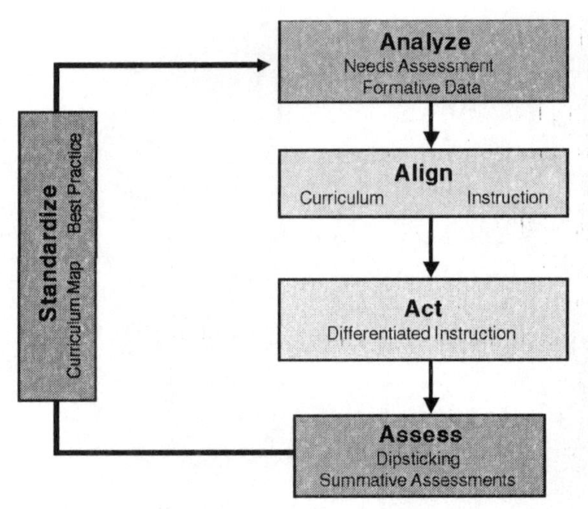

Figure 6.1. The A+ Approach

during Dr. Johnston's quarterly reviews with Mrs. Taylor that the summative teacher data are reviewed. They identify performance gaps and short-term deficiencies. For example, a student may have missed school because of illness for a few days and failed to catch up on critical instruction. Using this analysis the teacher can trace back to where the gap first occurred and provide remediation.

Bill knew how to analyze data very well. He had taken the district course on how to use data to inform instruction. Mrs. Taylor had also mentored him on more than one occasion how the process worked specifically for his students. He knew Malcolm had a significant gap in his learning that could be traced back to his previous school. It was not that the instruction was poor at the school but that the curriculum map was different and thus Malcolm missed some of the items that Blue Fields seventh graders covered.

The second A is *Align*. There are two components to this step—curriculum and instruction. Either or both may need adjustment. Bill had already been introduced to the Blue Fields curriculum maps. In fact he was asked to be part of a district team to help rewrite aspects of the map for the coming summer. He was highly flattered by this invitation. Mrs. Taylor told him that he had showed such a deep knowledge of math education at the middle level that his expertise was needed. Bill told himself all week that it did not got much better than that.

Mapped curriculum is the educational design focus at Blue Fields. At each grade level for each discipline, curriculum maps are laid out by content, process, and assessment objectives. They outline, for example, the math curriculum to be taught at the sixth grade level for each quarter of the year. The example in table 6.1 is a typical curriculum map for sixth grade math for the third quarter of the school year. In the content box is the essential question or the big idea of the curriculum for the quarter. Ten specific curriculum areas are listed here that students need to learn, and there are six activities for specific curriculum areas. In the product box is a project students will complete to demonstrate that they can apply the knowledge they have learned. In addition, there are other periodic assessments.

Table 6.1. Curriculum Map Sample

Content

Essential question: How are numbers used to measure time, space, distance, and change?

- Problem solving using fractions, decimals, percentages
- Commission, interest tax, percentage of increase/decrease
- Distance/rate/time (customary and metric measures)
- Geometry and measurement
- Problem solving with geometry
- Area, perimeter, volume
- Parallel, perpendicular, transverse
- Transformations
- Equivalent measurements
- Similarity and congruence

Process

- Solve problems using fractions.
- Solve problems using commission, interest tax, distance, rate, time, percentage of increase/decrease.
- Compare congruence and similarity.
- Find area, perimeter, volume.
- Use equivalent measurements.
- Use transformation in the coordinate plane.

Product

"A day in the life of . . . "

- Students collect data on the way they spend time and present it as fractions, decimals, percentages, and degrees.

Assessments

At first glance it seems that curriculum at Blue Fields is regimented and that teacher creativity is taken out of the classroom. Actually, quite the opposite takes place. The maps are designed by teachers working together with their colleagues at the same grade level and with colleagues at a grade below or above them. This way the map is aligned with the other grades as well. The curriculum maps at Blue Fields are not written and then placed in drawers. Rather, they are living documents, always being adjusted and refined based on assessment data received.

Bill had reviewed the eighth-grade curriculum map he was using and had also reviewed the seventh-grade map. He spoke with the seventh-grade teachers to ask about certain aspects of the map. Based on the quizzes he had given, he was fairly certain now that Malcolm had not been exposed to certain math content while in seventh grade at his previous school. He knew he could not adjust the curriculum map just for Malcolm's needs, so he had to look for another way to bring Malcolm up to the same level of content knowledge as others in the class.

He considered for a moment the second aspect of *Align*—instruction. This is the process where teachers are required to set goals to improve their delivery system for the curriculum. Each year at Blue Fields each teacher develops goals with his or her supervisor, usually the building principal. The goals are usually established by looking at the assessment results from the previous June, the status of the lag- and lead-goal results, and other measures. For some teachers it may be to take one of the five core in-service courses of the district. For others it may be to attend conferences, implement technology, or for the more veteran teachers to mentor one of newly hired teachers. The instructional goals for Bill for his first year were to learn the curriculum maps and attend two in-service courses, including the new-teacher orientation offered all year. Bill realized that alignment of the instructional goals or his delivery system was not going to help Malcolm achieve better.

Bill looked at the third A—*Act*. Here he knew he had the answer to Malcolm's problem. Teachers at Blue Fields are trained in differentiated instruction. They know that students have different learning styles and rates. In fact, at Bill's first interview with the superintendent this topic was mentioned. Bill was taught how to modify his lessons so that all learning groups in his class could complete the required work.

Lesson plans are written to include differentiated instruction. For example, in one of the sixth-grade classes at the school a social studies teacher had just completed a unit on Lewis and Clark's expedition through the land acquired in the Louisiana Purchase. As part of the lesson students were assigned to three groups. The groups were ability based and each group was given the same authentic journal entry from the expedition. The task for each group varied to reflect the ability of the group. For example:

Group C—Read the entry, identify five key discoveries, and write a two-page essay to answer the question "Was the Louisiana Purchase worth it?"

Group B—Read the entry, identify three key discoveries, and write a page-and-a-half essay to answer the question "Was the Louisiana Purchase worth it?"

Group A—Read the entry, identify two key discoveries, and write a one-page essay to answer the question "Was the Louisiana Purchase worth it?"

Bill knew Malcolm was going to have to master the math curriculum he had missed by changing schools. On the one hand, Bill did not want to punish Malcolm for this missed work. On the other, he knew that if Malcolm were going to master hands-on equations he would need to learn this missed work. He assigned Malcolm and a few other students who were having trouble to math lab. This was a special course taught by math teachers three times a week. Labs in the Blue Fields Middle School are built into the schedule to allow for differentiated learning. Some students need help in writing, some in reading, some in completing a particular project. Some students who qualify for special education need resource-room support. The labs are geared for each student need and therefore are designed to be small and flexible. Rarely is a student assigned to one curriculum area for the whole year. Students not needing remedial work are assigned to a lab that enhances the curriculum. All students at Blue Fields are challenged. Bill wrote a prescriptive goal to the math teacher in the math lab identifying the content and skill level Malcolm needed to master.

The fourth A is *Assess*. In this step the teachers conduct the actual assessments. These may be informal and formal, beginning at the individual student's achievement level. At Blue Fields it is called dip-sticking. These are quick assessments at the end of the lesson or week that give the teacher an idea of how well the students are doing. Summative assessments are given as well—state or national standardized assessments. Results are reported in a variety of formats. Parents at Blue Fields receive a report every four weeks. It is usually in the form of a report card or an interim report from the teacher. All data are reviewed quarterly by the administrative staff and in the summer by the board of education. Students who have special needs are assessed through the formal Child Study Teams. Results from the assessment phase are cycled back to the *Analyze* phase—step one.

Bill collected the informal assessments the lab math teacher had made on Malcolm's progress. Although Malcolm had been in the lab only three weeks, there was evidence of progress. The lab teacher and Bill sat together and analyzed the results. Bill made adjustments in this teaching for Malcolm based on the results. Bill began to see Malcolm's progress in the regular math class. Malcolm, he observed, was neither slow nor lazy.

That brings us to the last part of the process—*Standardize*. When goals are met, instructional strategies and curriculum design are standardized. Curriculum becomes integrated into the formal curriculum map for that grade or subject area. Instructional practices are adopted as best practices. These best practices are shared at grade and department meetings. The process is evidenced in the Blue Fields Performance Review Process illustrated in figure 3.2.

Bill learned from his experience with Malcolm. He knew he needed to preassess all of his students, particularly the new students, on their knowledge of math. He could not assume as he had done his first year at Blue Fields that every student enters his class with the same exposure to the same material. Some students will have gaps for a variety of reasons. Therefore, Bill standardized this A+ process map and developed pre-assessment materials not only for the eighth-grade course but also for the beginning of each new curriculum unit. This way he could differentiate his instruction for those students who had gaps in their knowledge.

Essential Question: Do Process Maps Stymie Creative Teachers?

If you ask excellent teachers you will find that they all have developed a formal or informal process map for their teaching. They may not know it or be able to articulate it, but if you ask them the steps they follow to assure that everyone in their class achieves, you will find at the core of their answer a process map. In Blue Fields' case, they referred to it as the A+ approach and it involved five steps. The number of steps is least important. At the core of effective educational design and delivery is a system. The system begins with data. The data identify the needs. The alignment is the process used to match the system's delivery to the needs identified by the data. The action taken is the result of the realignment. Every system needs to check itself to see if the action met the need. This has occurred when the data discovered is what you expected. Every system needs to highlight best practices of what worked and standardize it. The best practice needs to be celebrated and promoted throughout the system. The overall result is that the entire organization improves.

Process mapping can be used for support services as well as for educational design and delivery. By support we refer to the services that are used to maintain the educational system. In many districts it is the support services that are often seen as more important. It is the other way around. Typical examples of support services are the student cafeteria, business office functions, transportation, and technology support. By using process maps, a district can determine how effectively these services support the educational program.

A district should use survey results from faculty, parents, and students to help determine dissatisfaction in support services. These data can than be used to develop goals to improve the service, make it more cost-effective, connect it more closely to the educational program, or all of these. A plan of action is developed and a management plan and assessments are built in to determine whether refinements are needed or if the goal is met. Again, a performance review process can be used. Figure 6.2 shows a typical chart as an example of how the key support processes, requirements, measures, and inputs can be organized.

Support Process	*Key Requirement*	*Key Measure*
Purchasing	Timely payments	Cycle time
Payroll and benefits	Payroll accuracy Payroll on time	Payroll audit # of complaints
Duplicating/copying	Copying options Efficiency	Access to copies Cost
Technology, including computer support, voice mail, e-mail, Internet	Up time Accessibility	Up-time rate Voice mail/e-mail availability

Figure 6.2. Key Support Processes, Requirements, and Measures

7

GOOD ENOUGH NEVER IS

ORGANIZATIONAL PERFORMANCE RESULTS

Bill could not believe it was June already. Where did the year go? Today, his students were taking their final exam—and *he* was nervous. How could that be? The students were the ones who were supposed to be nervous. In his last district, he didn't remember feeling this anxious over a final exam. But, of course, he knew why.

In his last district, no one really cared about the results. At least not as they do at Blue Fields. As long as you didn't have an inordinately high number of failures, nobody paid much attention. If there was one thing he had learned at Blue Fields this year, it's that results count—a lot!

Bill watched as the students pored over the exam. He was proud of the test. He and his fellow eighth-grade math teachers had written it together with some input from the district's curriculum director. It was challenging but fair. He was anxious for them to do well and he was anxious for the results.

The two hours seemed to drag incessantly, but finally they were finished. Most finished before the allotted time, with a few going right to the bitter end, including Malcolm. Bill was hoping so much that Malcolm would do well. This was a tough year for both of them. Malcolm struggled with many of the concepts and Bill knew it affected his attitude. Bill tried many different interventions, including extra help sessions, additional time in math lab, and paying close attention to how Malcolm was keeping up in class. He was passing the course, but Bill also knew how Malcolm had difficulty with the sheer volume of material across the entire year, all of which was presented in this final exam.

Bill graded Malcolm's paper first. He had missed quite a few of the multiple choice questions, but aced three of the four full-problem proofs—the end result, a 79! Bill would have liked an 80, but was pleased that Malcolm had passed by a wide margin. Before moving on to the next paper, he took the time to analyze which questions Malcolm had missed. From the staff development course he took this year on using data to inform instruction, he learned how this information was invaluable to him as a teacher.

Sure enough, Malcolm's weak areas were in hands-on equations and the material from earlier in the year. No real surprises there, thought Bill. The question was, what could he have done differently to help Malcolm do better—to get that 80? Then, the thought jumped into his head, "Wow, I never used to think like this. In my last district, when a student did poorly, it was the student's fault. We never made the connections between student performance and teacher performance." Bill realized this was yet another epiphany for him, one of many he had come to experience during this incredibly challenging year at Blue Fields.

The following afternoon, Bill arrived for his meeting with Mrs. Taylor. At the close of final exams, she met with all of the new teachers to go over their results. This was no surprise to Bill. He was informed of the procedure much earlier in the year and had talked to some of the other teachers about it, so he had done his homework. He had broken down all of his students' test grades by question, called a gap analysis—again, something he had learned in the staff development course. This way, he could determine if there were one or more areas that a disproportionate number of his students missed. If that was the case, then clearly he was not effective in teaching those concepts.

While the data did not seem to reveal any specific areas of overall weakness, it did suggest weakness in those areas taught earlier in the school year. Bill thought about the reviews he had conducted and how he could have tackled this better. His thoughts were interrupted by Mrs. Taylor inviting him into her office.

"Well, William," she began. "Congratulations on completing your first year at Blue Fields."

"Thank you," he replied. "I have to say, it has been an incredible year. I never realized how much I didn't know about teaching and learning. I thought I was set to go once I graduated from teaching school," he admitted.

"Most teachers do. I certainly did way back in the dark ages," she laughed. "But your open acknowledgment of how much you still have to learn is really the key for us in this district," she said. "Now, let's get down to business."

For the next half hour, she went over Bill's students' results. Her analysis went much farther than Bill's, but she was pleased to see he had done the gap analysis on the final exam and considered improvements in his strategies for next year. She showed Bill comparisons between his different period classes and comparisons with the other teachers teaching the same course, as well as all of the other teachers in the math department. They looked at comparisons between his male and female students and they looked at the performance of his more challenged learners. They compared first-quarter grades with mid-terms and final exams, looking for trend lines.

Bill was blown away. He had never seen anything like this. There was so much to absorb. From her experience, Eva Taylor knew how overwhelming this could be the first time around. "So, William, now you can see what we mean when we talk about the importance of data," she said.

He tried not to appear overwhelmed. "You can say that again," he responded. "There is so much information here. I really need to take some time to absorb it all," he hedged.

"Of course you do," she replied. "That is one reason why you have a ten-week summer recess," she laughed. "All kidding aside, that is exactly what you need to do next. Take the time to review all of this more thoroughly. When we return in the fall, you and I will meet again. We will use this information to plan your professional goals for next year."

Bill thought about Mrs. Taylor. He had such respect for how much she knew about teaching and learning. He was grateful for her support but also realized that it was something he had to earn through his attitude and his commitment. "I look forward to that," he said, and he meant it. "Have a great summer and thank you for everything," he said and shook her hand.

There never seemed to be enough time. Eva Taylor took one last look at her data report. Today began the two-day Administrative Retreat the superintendent held each year within ten days after the close of school.

During these two days, the central office administrators and building principals carefully reviewed performance results across the entire district. They looked at student performance and participation, faculty and staff performance, satisfaction data, budgetary and fiscal data, and overall organizational-system results.

These two days were the prelude to the Blue Fields Administrative Advance, held later in the summer. During the advance, the central office administrators and building principals planned their course for the coming year, based on the results from the prior year.

Eva had her data all in order. Over the years, she had learned how important it was to really know and understand her results. As the middle school principal, she was the one ultimately responsible for how well the sixth-, seventh-, and eighth-grade students performed. She was not allowed to blame it on the teachers or the parents or the students. She was the instructional leader for middle-level education, and if it wasn't working, she was accountable for fixing it.

Along with her fellow administrators, she had already submitted the hard copies of the data, along with her preliminary analysis, to her assistant superintendent. The assistant superintendent then assembled all of the results into one document and distributed it to everyone in advance to review before the retreat.

While not all of the district year-end data were final, they still had so much to review. First and foremost was looking at the results based on their goals for the past year. The administrative team sets performance targets at the beginning of each year in specific areas of their program they are looking to improve. They then outline projects or actions they will take to reach these new targets.

For this past year, improving eighth-grade math performance was one of the district's lead goals. Lead goals are short-term goals that serve as predictors for long-term, end-result goals, called lag goals. In this case, there was a clear relationship between how well students did in eighth-grade math and how successful they were in meeting the mathematics requirements for graduation. As a result, Eva Taylor made eighth-grade math a priority this year.

This was particularly challenging since one of her three eighth-grade math teachers was new. There is always concern when an experienced, proven veteran teacher retires and a new, less experienced teacher comes on board. She spent extra time with William, observed his teaching four times, and thoroughly reviewed his students' grades each quarter. She assigned him a veteran teacher to mentor him and also conferred with the curriculum director and assistant superintendent who were teaching the new-teacher inservice course to see how he was doing.

All of this focus paid off. This year's eighth-grade math results improved nine percent over last year. The percentage of students passing the course rose from 83 percent to 91 percent and the percentage of students achieving mastery (85 percent or better) rose from 38 percent to 46 percent. Eva was both pleased and proud to share the results with her team.

At the same time, however, she knew that 91 percent was not good enough. She found herself already thinking about what she would do differently next year to close the gap to 100 percent. The 9 percent that were not passing were truly some of the most challenged learners in the school—most of them classified as special education. But the Blue Fields mission is that *every* child can and will learn. She knew she had her work cut out for her.

That was confirmed when the board of education held their review later after the administrative advance. As the governing body of the school district, the board reviews and approves the proposed lag goals, lead goals, and projects each year. As does everyone else at Blue Fields, they carefully consider the results of the prior year in their review.

Dr. Johnston, the assistant superintendent, and the business manager comb through all of the data, ranking the long-term, big-picture lag results, as well as the areas of concern. If there was one thing Dr. Johnston had learned about this continuous-improvement model, it was that you could drown in the data, and there were a number of times when he almost did.

To survive, they learned they needed to make priorities. Not everyone needed to look at every piece of data. For example, the board of education did not need to know how many of William's students got question 4 wrong on the final exam. William needed to know that. Mrs. Taylor and Dr. Johnston needed to know how William's students were doing compared with the other eighth-grade math teachers' students. And the board of education needed to know if the eighth-grade math program was adequately preparing students for success in high school.

In addition to academic results, the board looked at performance measures for their other two district goals—perception and cost-efficiency.

Again, their concern was not so much with the detail, such as how many dollars were saved by converting to an energy-efficient light bulb. As the governing body for the education system in their community, they spent more time on the end results. Most importantly, they used these results to set the stage for new and higher performance. Good enough never is!

Essential Question: How Do We Know When the Results Are Good?

Usually when a teacher or a school district collects data it ends up with too much data. They have so much, in fact, that they do not know how to use it. Often you will hear a school administrator say about data, "Oh, we are into data." What exactly this means is unclear. But often it means that the person collects a lot of data, looks at some of it, analyzes even less, and uses very little.

The first step in determining if the data are good is to determine which of the data are more important than other data. It is best to separate the data into cluster groupings in terms of relevance. The use of the Balanced Scorecard illustrated in chapter 5 serves this purpose. Data collected on the lag goals are the most important. So these data need to be charted first. In our story, Malcolm's final grade was an important indicator of success, so it needs to be charted.

The next step in determining if the data are good is to organize the data selected in step one according to a certain format. All data need to be represented by trends. This means the direction of the results and the rate of change need to be represented. Hopefully, the trend lines move in a positive fashion. If your goal is to increase achievement, for example, the trend needs to go up. If you want to reduce costs in certain areas, you would want the trend to go down. At a minimum, three data points are needed to show a trend; ideally, five to seven.

Next come the performance levels on a measurement scale. In Malcolm's case the teacher was measuring percentage of correct answers on the final math exam. However, the teacher could have used other measures such as raw score, scaled scores, or percentiles as measurement. Whatever is chosen, the measurement needs to be consistent and show trends.

All data need to be compared with benchmark data. In the case of Malcolm, the increase in achievement, as measured by the percent of correct answers on the exam, needs to be compared with the performance measures of other students in the class. This comparison is critical because it shows whether the goal was achieved because of an intervention strategy or some other factor. For example, was Malcolm's increase in the math exam results due to the intervention strategies of the teacher or to some outside factor such as the exam being easier? If the exam were easier, then all of the students would show improvement similar to Malcolm's.

So for us to determine if Malcolm's score was good, we need to look at trends, measurement, and comparisons.

If we charted Malcolm's progress using these three factors the result would be as shown in figure 7.1.

The teacher chose a positive measurement, grade on final exam, and a trend line of the four, separate quarter grades, which showed positive gain, and a comparison with the average of the entire class grades over the same time. It is clear that Malcolm's grades improved steadily over time compared with those of the entire class. On the final exam, he scored virtually the same, 79 percent compared with 80 percent for the entire class.

We can draw the conclusion from this that the results are good.

The use of graphs and tables are important in displaying the results, especially if your goal is to convince another that the data are good. Most people do not want to read through a long discourse on data. They prefer to view it in a format that is easy to read. The graph in Malcolm's case illustrates how multiple measures can be displayed in a positive fashion.

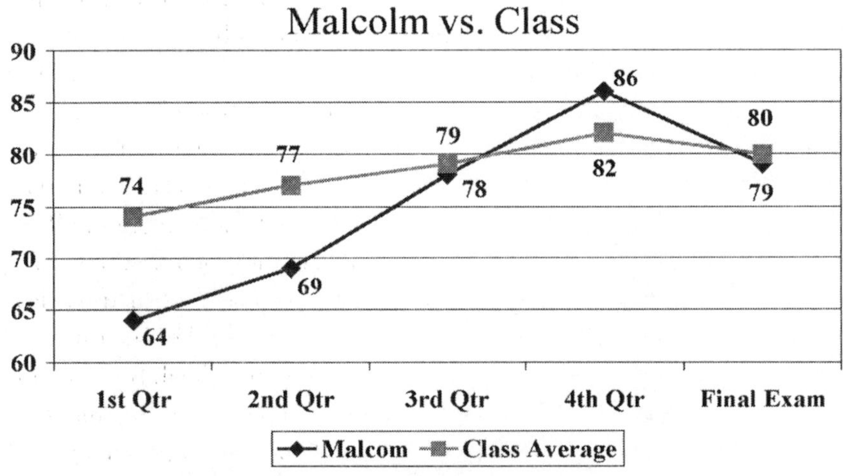

Figure 7.1. Malcolm vs. Class Quarterly and Exam Grades

Comparative data are important because they provide a benchmark for our progress. The term comes from woodworking: shops made marks on the bench that indicated the point of excellence in measuring, cutting, or assembling. The Baldrige award program requires that comparative data be the best in class. The benchmark then becomes a system of best practice that you strive to meet or beat. If your trend-line data run parallel to that of the benchmark data over time, then it could be said there is no evidence of continuous improvement. If your trend line moves in a positive direction toward beating the benchmark point, then you can say that the program is working. In most Baldrige organizations, it is important to have world-class results, so the goal is to beat the benchmark.

In our case, Bill is not trying to have Malcolm become a world-class eighth-grade math student. Nor is the goal to receive a better grade than that of the brightest student in the class. Rather, we have seen that Bill has set as his goal to have Malcolm pass the course. To this end he chose the class average as a comparative benchmark.

It is important to remember that the purpose of using benchmarks is to drive you to produce the same results as those of the best. Usually this would require that you not only benchmark the data but also the best practices of doing things. The goal would be to adopt the practices that produced these positive results.

The use of comparative data can also help explain unexpectedly poor results. For example, in figure 7.2 you can see the Blue Fields School District grade four English language-arts test results over a six-year period.

For the first three years, Blue Fields had results similar to those of the best school in the state. Almost 100 percent of the students passed the exam. Yet, in year four, the district results plunged because of the introduction by the state of a more rigorous, longer exam. This could have been a disaster for Blue Fields to report except that the benchmark district data fell as well. In the last two years, Blue Fields made steady progress on improving student achievement. Although it did not reach its previous goal of almost 100 percent passing the exam, it did beat the benchmark district and does show a positive upward trend.

A more complicated version of how to demonstrate if data are good is to show that a practice is not only improving a factor, but that it is having a positive effect on another factor.

An example would be the study of how Blue Fields' technology program improved over time and as a result both the faculty and the student satisfaction rate improved as well. In figure 7.3 the percentage of time a district's computer

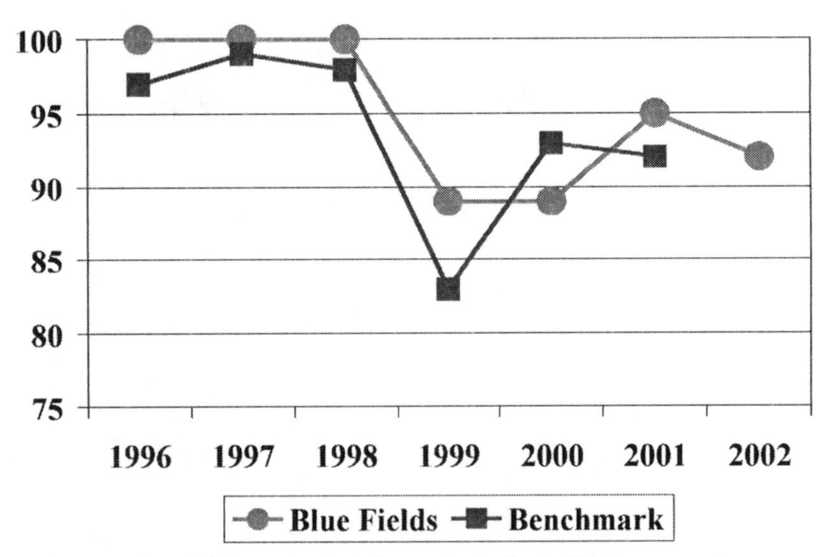

Figure 7.2. Blue Fields vs. Benchmark Fourth-Grade English Language Arts

servers were operating (up time) is displayed as improving over time. The trend lines are up. In addition, the faculty and student satisfaction rates for technology use have also moved up. One can draw the conclusion that the district's efforts to improve its technology services had direct, positive effect on student and faculty feelings about the district. Again, this is an example of good data.

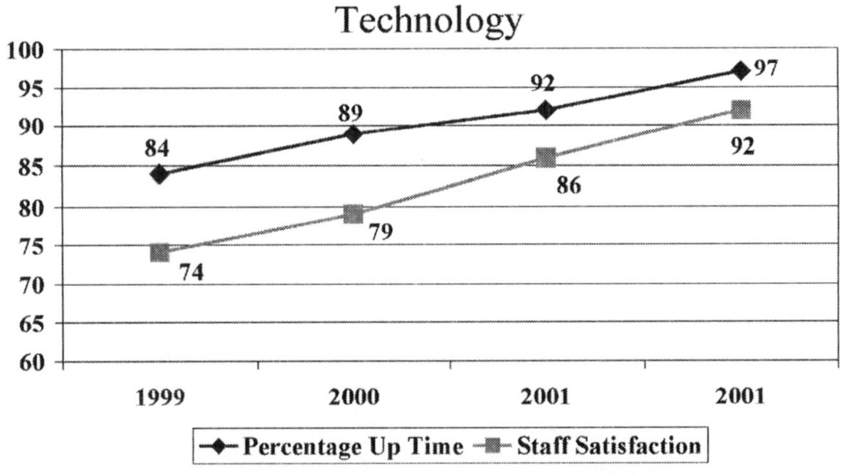

Figure 7.3. Comparative Analysis: Technology and Staff Satisfaction

EPILOGUE

So What Happened to Malcolm and Bill?

Malcolm advanced from middle school and is now a senior in Blue Fields High School. He maintains a B+ average, is applying for college, and is a member of the varsity soccer team. Jeannie, his mom, is so glad he did not play football, despite all the efforts of the coach to get him to play. In math he is taking precalculus. This may seem like a miracle compared with where he was in eighth grade, only five years ago. Yet Malcolm worked hard once he saw that he could achieve. He was shown that he was not dumb in math. In eighth grade he needed to relearn things and he needed to cover material he had not been taught before. In addition, he worked hard by attending extra classes. As he began to improve, he gained self-confidence and believed what his teacher was saying—that he could do it.

As for Bill, the rookie teacher, he is now the senior member of the math department in the middle school. How could this happen? Given colleagues' absences for maternity leaves and a retirement incentive, Bill quickly rose through the ranks. This was both good and bad for him. While he learned how to use data to inform instruction and was able to improve the achievement of many students, like Malcolm he still needs to grow professionally.

What is important is that Bill sees this and has not given up learning. He feels empowered in the school because he has a say in how things are done. He has become quite competent in analyzing achievement data. He does not feel the district uses data to punish him but rather as a means for him to improve his teaching. Because of this culture, Bill is willing to take more risks and spend more time with students like Malcolm. He has seen the results of his efforts make a difference and he is convinced more students can be helped.

The principal, Eva Taylor, continues to be the principal. She jokes about how she has hired so many young teachers that she feels like a mom. In fact, Eva has hired quite well. Her new teachers are bright and eager and they care about students. She is training them as she did Malcolm. Because of the large number of new people and the growing lack of experienced mentors, Eva persuaded the superintendent, Dr. Johnston, to hire a part-time self-developer for the school. As a result, the middle school has an experienced teacher who works with other teachers to map curriculum, analyze data, and differentiate instruction. She provides the peer critiques that teachers like Bill need if they are to grow professionally. It is the clear vision of Eva that allowed this critical component of instruction to be available. Eva knows her building and staff are student-centered and professional. The Blue Fields Middle School will be a school of excellence for years to come. And teachers like Bill will be attracted to the school because they know they can grow professionally and be better. Parents in the district, like Jeannie, will be confident that the school more than meets the needs of their children. And for the Malcolms of the district, there is a feeling and knowledge that the district places them first. Students indeed are the satisfied customers.

District families without school-age children have also benefited from the Blue Fields ways. Since they began using a continuous-improvement approach to manage their district, administrators have seen the number of families considering moving into the district increase dramatically. This is reinforced by local realtors who report that home values have more than doubled over the past five years. They complain that there is never enough inventory for the long list of clients they have who want a home in the Blue Fields School District.

In fact, pretty much everyone in the county knows of the Blue Fields success. Whenever the state education department releases the latest test results, the local newspaper runs a full spread with all of the districts' scores laid out in comparison tables and graphs. Years ago, Blue Fields results usually fell somewhere in the middle of the pack. But in more recent years, they typically are the highest. Administrators hear from their colleagues in other districts that "Blue Fields is the district to chase."

While this pleases Dr. Johnston and Mrs. Taylor and Bill and all of the faculty and staff, it has other positive effects as well. The community as a whole feels good about their school district. They are proud to say that their children attend school at Blue Fields. More importantly, they support their schools. Whether it's to volunteer for a school function, come out to see a play or football game, buy an ad in the yearbook, or vote yes on a bond issue, local residents and businesses are there supporting Blue Fields.

And while the board of education and administration are thankful for this, they also know that they cannot take it for granted. They cannot stop trying to do better for their students. Good enough never is.

APPENDIX A

It's Not Continuous Improvement When . . .

It's not continuous improvement when

- You adopt a new program because it worked well in another district (best practice) but has no relation to your district's assessed needs, goals, or plans.
- You immediately jump to the solution to the problem without taking the time to find out why the problem happened in the first place.
- You proudly present all of your year-end data to your school board and then place it on the shelf with all of the other year-end data from prior years, never to be looked at again.
- Your mission statement is so long that you need to read it to remind yourself of what it says.
- You spend big dollars training everyone in your district on quality and quality tools and then keep doing everything the same way you always have. You just use different words for it.
- Your high school teachers never talk to your middle school teachers and your middle school teachers never talk to your elementary school teachers.
- Your high school principal never talks to your middle school principal and your middle school principal never talks to your elementary school principal.

- You conduct satisfaction surveys and see that your parents rank communication low. You decide to beef up the district web page. The following year, they still rate communication low.
- Whenever you start talking about it, everyone nods politely (or rolls their eyes) and then keeps on doing what they have always done.
- Everybody is doing it but the superintendent.

APPENDIX B

How to Get Started

This section is divided into two parts. The first is a question-and-answer format. The second will help you get started.

QUESTION AND ANSWER

We are frequently asked how we got started. Listed here are some of the more common questions.

What Is the Motivation to Get Involved with Baldrige?

We advise not getting involved to win the award. The award is wonderful and will be a great recognition for any district's hard work. The value in Baldrige is in the process. The process is so strong that it will improve the district over time—hence, continuous improvement. One of the key motivators is witnessing the advance in student achievement that results because you have implemented the process. Other areas that are chosen for improvement will advance as well. Looking forward to the feedback report you will receive after submitting an application is also motivating. This is a written report of about fifty pages compiled by experts. It will list your organization's strengths and areas for growth based on the seven Baldrige criteria. Reviewing the feedback and implementing its suggestions will drive the district's improvement.

How Do You Decide Students Are the Customers?

One of the initial tasks of any organization is to determine why it exists. You can say that the district or school serves multiple customers: parents, taxpayers, and employees as well as students. This is correct. But it is critical that students be singled out as *the* customer. The other groups are important, but they are stakeholders. No school would be in existence if the students did not exist. When you go shopping in any store you expect to be treated as the customer. You do not expect the clerk, the owner, or the stockholder to be the customer. You are the only customer. Only when students are so identified can the organization then develop plans and goals built primarily on serving student needs.

How Do You Overcome Skepticism?

Let's face it. Most school employees have seen programs come and go and often come back again. Each is sold as the answer to the problem. The cycle is the same. The program does not work and is replaced with another. Teachers are used to curriculum-of-the-month-type programming. Nothing improves, suspicion grows, and trust in administration diminishes. The way to sell Baldrige is not to sell it. The role of administration is to model. The administration needs to be seen as acting as if students are the customers, employees are valued, and parents are welcome. Teachers do not need to learn all the Baldrige jargon. They need to be heard, supported, and provided with the means for professional development. The district improvement as a result of using Baldrige needs to be celebrated. Once student achievement improves, skepticism will disappear.

How Do You Get Teachers to Buy In?

If you do not agree with the answer to the question about overcoming skepticism you will never get teachers to buy in. Staff—teachers as well as other staff—need to be involved from the beginning. They should feel as though Baldrige is something they can do. The superintendent has to *do* Baldrige, not just talk Baldrige.

Is Writing the Application Hard?

Yes. Do not expect to complete it in a few months. Divide the chapters into sections and appoint chapter champions to master and collect data on the criteria. Appoint one person to write the main part of the application. The person should be an employee who has a big-picture view of the organization and is familiar with the unique vocabulary of continuous improvement. Appoint one person to collect the data for the results chapter, the seventh Baldrige criterion.

Write drafts upon drafts and have employees who are not part of the team review it with a fresh eye for content and grammar.

Can You Be Involved in Baldrige if the Superintendent Is Not?

No. Leadership is key and the boss needs to model the process.

WHERE TO START?

Orient

The senior leadership of the district needs to lead the journey. The first step in the process of continuous improvement is to cultivate awareness of what the process entails and the specific format and criteria that are addressed in the journey. There are many conferences at the national, state, and regional levels that provide specific information on continuous improvement and the Baldrige process. Conferences conducted by the National Malcolm Baldrige Quality Program can be found at their website, www.baldrige.nist.gov. Many states have very strong continuous-improvement award programs that are modeled after the Baldrige process. These are a good first step. They are usually listed on state websites. It is important that a study team be formed consisting of administration, union leaders, and other key staff. The focus of the team is to decide if the process is worth the end result. The team does not need to figure out the details at this point. They need to decide if there is value in beginning the process.

Describe

Baldrige recommends that the team complete an organizational profile of the district or school. This is a snapshot of the district and serves as a form of self-assessment. The complete questions as well as the whole Baldrige application can be found in the *Education Criteria for Performance Excellence*, a publication available at www.baldrige.nist.gov through the National Malcolm Baldrige Quality Program. There are two statements to be completed.

- Describe your organization's environment and your key relationships with students, stakeholders, suppliers, and other partners. In this statement describe your main programs, services, culture, mission, values, and purpose. Describe the faculty by its level of experience and education, staff development opportunities, and health and safety requirements. Also include the major technologies, equipment, facilities that you use, and the regulations under which you operate. List your boundaries and restrictions. List governance and reporting relationships among key administrators, key student and stakeholder groups, and market focus. Include your partners and suppliers and how you communicate to all stakeholders.
- Describe your organization's competitive environment, your key strategic challenges, and your system for performance improvement. For your competitive position, describe your market and list competitors. What makes you different from others and what changes are going on to make you more competitive? Where do you get key comparative data and are there limitations on securing these data? List your strategic challenges in learning, human resources, community, and operations. How you plan to improve should be described, as well as your approach to organizational learning and sharing knowledge within the organization.

Completing these statements will help you get used to the format of the Baldrige application. At first it may seem as though the answers are common knowledge to all. But you will find that not everyone knows the same thing and many on the team have different understandings of the organization. Use the written answers as part of an administrative workshop to verify the content.

List those areas where there is disagreement or lack of full knowledge.

Communicate

The governing board of the school district needs to be apprised of the process that the senior administration is undertaking. They do not need to understand the whole process but their commitment is necessary. This sends a strong message to the staff and community that a formal continuous-improvement journey is beginning. A formal presentation at a board meeting or for a PTA group would help muster support.

The question is what to tell the district staff. It is important to remember that Baldrige is an *organizational* improvement process. It is not a process that starts with changing classrooms. It is important to avoid early skepticism of the process by announcing how it is going to change the district 180 degrees. What is important is to inform the staff that the Baldrige process is going to change the administration. Specifically, administrators will be using data to make decisions based on a systematic process. Faculty and staff input and involvement are critical but they should be in the form of collaboration and trust, not top-down orders. The staff should be told that the administration would like its help in discovering the best practices in the classrooms and finding a way to disseminate the practices throughout the district. The staff needs assurance from administration that the process will improve student achievement because they will be involved in it. The key here is that the staff feels genuinely that the process of continuous improvement is not being done to them but is being done *by* them.

Team Baldrige

A formal team of administrators, staff, and, where relevant, parents should be formed to direct the process. The initial planning team needs to be expanded based on the scope of the project being undertaken. All team members need to become aware of the Baldrige process. Trips to districts using the process or national, state, or regional conventions are helpful. A consultant can also be used at this level to help the team with its tasks and understanding of the process.

Scope

Next, decide what part of your district or organization should be involved. This is an important decision because it determines the scope of the Baldrige process implementation. You can start with a grade level, a school, a department, or the entire district. The key to making this decision is how much time and staff you can devote to implementing Baldrige. You may want to complete the Baldrige self-assessment in appendix C on various subunits and, based on scores, then decide which to begin with. If you are doing the full organization, the self-assessment is a good introduction.

Data

Once the scope is decided you need to determine what kind of data you have already collected and what kind of data need to be collected. To begin, make a list of all the data that the district collects. Decide which support the district mission directly and which data are secondary. For example, if you have data on eleventh-grade English exams and data on fourth-grade and eighth-grade English language arts exams you will decide that the eleventh-grade data come first because they are closer to the exit graduation date. The fourth- and eighth-grade data become supportive in that they provide a line of sight to the eleventh-grade performance. Some of the data a district collects are less important than others.

In addition, the format of how the data are collected needs to be decided. By this we mean the time line (by quarter, semester, yearly, biannual, etc.), who is responsible for collecting the data, and the graphic organizer to be used (graph, spread sheet, percentiles, standardized scores, etc.).

Champions

The task of implementing Baldrige needs to be divided among the staff. Staff involvement and empowerment are the keys to making this work. Since there are seven criteria in Baldrige, there should be one or two chapter champions who know the criteria in detail and who are capable of explaining each criterion's link to the other categories. One champion on each team should have knowledge of the whole organization, so school administrators are common choices. However, teachers can be part of any champion team to ensure teacher empowerment and involvement from the start.

Format

What is the style of the report to be made? Should it be in bullets, short statements, oral reports, or full paragraphs? The last one is the hardest and requires some writing skill. Usually the chapter champions begin by sitting down and using a bullet format to first answer the criteria. From there a more detailed written response can be made. The whole group may want to look at the seven-bullet response format first to help develop the big picture and to assure that the answers are geared to the organizational profile completed earlier.

Action Plan

Based on the responses to the seven criteria the team can develop action plans. First, it needs to identify which items are strengths for each criterion. For example, under Leadership the team may want to identify which items showed that the organization met the criteria fully. There will be other criteria sections that show few responses or even responses that conflict with each other. For example, one group may state there is a strong strategic plan and another state there is little evidence that a planning process is in place. As the list of opportunities for improvement grows, the team needs to review these items to determine whether the organization has steps in place to answer the criteria but the team missed in its list. For those that are confusing, the team will need to explore the item further.

The team is now ready to develop action plans. It is best to look at each criterion and count the number of responses listed or, if you are using the self-assessment listed in appendix C, locate which criterion has the most "strongly disagree" responses. A discussion among the leadership should analyze the data and decide which needs to be addressed first. For example, if the self-assessment item 1g, "My organization asks what I think," has a high number of "strongly disagree" responses, an action plan to develop a survey instrument may be a solution. Or, for example, a district may need to develop a complaint log to answer the question of how it monitors student, staff, and stakeholder satisfaction. A complete action plan with an implementation team needs to be established. Again, this is a good area to involve other district staff as a way to help understand Baldrige. For those items that are confusing, the team may want to hire a consultant. For example, under the question of how a district describes its processes for handling work-order requests, a consultant may be needed to work with the clerical staff on how to develop a process map.

Share

The team needs to share its work and feedback with a larger audience to ensure that it is on track and that its efforts are recognized. While some may say it is too early and that the team needs to collect more facts, a larger part of the organization's staff needs to be involved to address these needs. To limit the process to the team will ensure that any changes are not organizational changes but paper changes.

Evaluate

The process of implementing Baldrige needs to be evaluated at this point. The team needs to ask itself if the activities it is using are working and if not, why. The format for reporting may need lengthening. Are the right data available in the right format?

Are the champions appropriately assigned? Are the appropriate staff involved? Should the teams be expanded? What kind of feedback was received in the sharing process? Can it be incorporated to make the process better?

Recycle

The whole process needs to begin again, hence, continuous improvement. There should be enough results the first year to be quantifiable and sustain the belief that the process can work. The self-assessment guide in appendix C can be given again to see if there is perceptible improvement in the scores. But the journey is a long one and really never is completed. The cycle of getting started just continues as the district improves over time.

APPENDIX C

Are We Making Progress?

(Publication of the Baldrige National Quality Program)

The Baldrige award program has developed a self-assessment checklist that can be used to analyze at least at the initial level where a school or a school district rates on the seven Baldrige categories. There are 40 statements on the checklist that relate directly to the criteria specified in the Baldrige application. The difference here is that the checklist is a rating while the application process is a written narrative.

Our recommendation is to give the checklist to the senior leaders in your school or school district. Have them rate each statement in the box that best matches how they feel: (strongly disagree, disagree, neither agree or disagree, agree, strongly agree). Remind them you are not looking at individual responses but are using the information from the whole group to make decisions. It should take a person about 10 to 15 minutes to complete the questionnaire. The results should be shared with those who took the survey. The next step would be to follow the Getting-Started Plan in appendix B.

AN ASSESSMENT TOOL FROM THE BALDRIGE NATIONAL QUALITY PROGRAM

- This new, easy-to-use questionnaire can help you assess how your organization is performing and learn what can be improved.

- We encourage you to photocopy it and distribute it to your employees, your managers and supervisors, or your senior leadership team.
- You can modify the questionnaire to address your specific needs (e.g., add questions, use language specific to your organization).
- You also can download an electronic version of the questionnaire from the Baldrige National Quality Program web site at www.quality.nist.gov

Message to Leaders

In today's environment, if you are standing still you are falling behind. Making the right decisions at the right time is critical. Following through on those decisions is challenging. In a survey of a broad cross section of CEOs, the Malcolm Baldrige Foundation learned that CEOs believed deploying strategy is three times more difficult than developing strategy. If deployment is so challenging, the questions are, Are you making progress? How do you know?

- Are your vision, mission, values, and plans being deployed? How do you know?
- Are they understood by your leadership team? How do you know?
- Are they understood by all employees? How do you know?
- Are your communications effective? How do you know?
- Is the message being well received? How do you know?

Are We Making Progress? is designed to help you know. It provides a tool for you to see if your perceptions agree with those of your employees. It will help you focus your improvements and communication efforts on areas needing the most attention. For organizations that have been using the Baldrige Criteria for Performance Excellence, the questionnaire is conveniently organized by the seven criteria categories. For those who haven't been using the Baldrige Criteria, turning to those criteria categories where this questionnaire identifies opportunities for improvement may help you identify some key ideas for making improvements.

It is never too soon to start improving openness and communication. Ask your employees their opinions. They will appreciate the opportunity—and the organization will benefit from their response!

Are We Making Progress? Questionnaire

Your opinion is important to us. There are 40 statements below. For each statement, check the box that best matches how you feel (strongly disagree, disagree, neither agree nor disagree, agree, strongly agree). How you feel will help us decide where we most need to improve. We will not be looking at individual responses but will use the information from our whole group to make decisions. It should take you about 10 to 15 minutes to complete this questionnaire.

Senior leaders, please fill in the following information:

____

Name of organization or unit being discussed

Category 1: Leadership

1a: I know my organization's mission (what it is trying to accomplish).
1b: My senior (top) leaders use our organization's values to guide us.
1c: My senior leaders create a work environment that helps me do my job.
1d: My organization's leaders share information about the organization.
1e: My senior leaders encourage learning that will help me advance in my career.
1f: My organization lets me know what it thinks is most important.
1g: My organization asks what I think.

Category 2: Strategic Planning

2a: As it plans for the future, my organization asks for my ideas.
2b: I know the parts of my organization's plans that will affect me and my work.
2c: I know how to tell if we are making progress on my work group's part of the plan.

Category 3: Customer and Market Focus

3a: I know who my most important customers are.
3b: I keep in touch with my customers.
3c: My customers tell me what they need and want.
3d: I ask if my customers are satisfied or dissatisfied with my work.
3e: I am allowed to make decisions to solve problems for my customers.

Category 4: Information and Analysis

4a: I know how to measure the quality of my work.
4b: I know how to analyze (review) the quality of my work to see if changes are needed.
4c: I use these analyses for making decisions about my work.
4d: I know how the measures I use in my work fit into the organization's overall measures of improvement.
4e: I get all the important information I need to do my work.
4f: I get the information I need to know about how my organization is doing.

Category 5: Human Resource Focus

5a: I can make changes that will improve my work.
5b: The people I work with cooperate and work as a team.
5c: My boss encourages me to develop my job skills so I can advance in my career.
5d: I am recognized for my work.
5e: I have a safe workplace.
5f: My boss and my organization care about me.

Category 6: Process Management

6a: I can get everything I need to do my job.
6b: I collect information (data) about the quality of my work.

6c: We have good processes for doing our work.
6d: I have control over my work processes.

Category 7: Business Results

7a: My customers are satisfied with my work.
7b: My work products meet all requirements.
7c: I know how well my organization is doing financially.
7d: My organization uses my time and talents well.
7e: My organization removes things that get in the way of progress.
7f: My organization obeys laws and regulations.
7g: My organization has high standards and ethics.
7h: My organization helps my community.
7i: I am satisfied with my job.

Would you like to give more information about any of your responses? Please include the number of the statement (for example, 2a or 7d) you are discussing.

ABOUT THE AUTHORS

Richard E. Maurer, Ph.D., is the superintendent of schools of the Pearl River School District and a 2001 Malcolm Baldrige National Quality Award winner. He has served in education for more than thirty years, nine as superintendent, is the author of five previous books, and has taught graduate education classes.

Sandra Cokeley Pedersen authored the 2001 Malcolm Baldrige National Quality Award application for the Pearl River School District, one of the first three education recipients. As the district's director of quality and community relations, she has been driving continuous improvement at Pearl River since 1992.